BECOMING
HEART
SISTERS

A Bible Study on Authentic Friendships

NATALIE CHAMBERS SNAPP

Abingdon Women / Nashville

Becoming Heart Sisters
A Bible Study on Authentic Friendships

19 20 21 22 23 24 25 26 — 10 9 8 7 6 5
MANUFACTURED IN THE UNITED STATES OF AMERICA

CONTENTS

ABOUT THE AUTHOR

Natalie Chambers Snapp is an author, blogger, and speaker who describes herself first and foremost as a follower of Jesus, then wife to Jason, and mom to one spunky daughter and two spirited sons with a whole lot of energy. Not choosing to follow Jesus until the age of twenty-seven, she is passionate about sharing the grace, mercy, and truth of God's love regardless of your track record. Her authentic approach to life and faith is both refreshing and endearing. She is the author of *Heart Sisters: Be the Friend You Want to Have* and has written for various blogs and online devotionals, including Proverbs 31, as well as The Mothers of Boys Society, Whatever Girls Ministry, and Group Publishing. She lives in the Midwest with her crew and writes about faith in the everyday mundane.

Follow Natalie:

Twitter	@NatalieSnapp
Instagram	@nataliesnapp
Facebook	@AuthorNatalieSnapp
Blog	NatalieSnapp.com
	(check here for event dates and booking information)

INTRODUCTION

In today's world of technological advancements, we are more connected than ever before, but we struggle to *feel* connected. From the false intimacy of social media to our fast-paced lifestyles and increased mobility that results in the transplanting of families, there are many challenges to developing meaningful friendships today. If that isn't enough to keep us from seeking and investing in genuine relationships, there often is another challenge: conflict.

Conflict is a common obstacle for many of us when it comes to navigating friendships with other women. As I have conducted research for a book and now this study on friendship, so many women have sent me heartfelt messages filled with sadness, frustration, and despair over friend breakups and other relational conflict. When we have been hurt in relationships, we can be tempted to give up on friendship and "go it alone." I've been there myself.

There was a time when I told God that I was done with female friends, reassuring myself that my family would be enough because it was just too difficult (and painful) to have girlfriends. The challenges and conflicts I had experienced in past relationships—in addition to the everyday obstacles of a busy life and full schedule—made me reluctant to take risks and try again. But deep down, I knew I needed girlfriends. I knew God created us for relationship—with Himself and with other people—and I knew this includes relationships with other women. I knew that friendships with other women are as important to our mental, physical, and spiritual health as rest, exercise, and prayer. So I cautiously stuck my toes in the waters of friendship again, and with God's help and the guidance of the Scriptures, I rediscovered how to cultivate authentic friendships.

I can honestly say that these authentic relationships with other women are one of the richest blessings I've ever received from God. I adore my husband, and my children are proof of God's goodness and mercy; but there is no substitute for the gift of genuine girlfriends. I call them "Heart Sisters"—those friends who carry me when I can't walk, speak truth when I'm believing lies, and make me laugh when all I want to do is cry. Though we are not related by blood, we are like family—sisters united by a deep connection of the heart.

Heart Sisters truly are a "good and perfect gift...from the Father" (James 1:17 NIV), and He wants to bless each and every one of us with this gift. Whether you are longing to have authentic friendships of your own, struggling to balance friendship with everyday life, navigating a hurt or conflict with a friend, or simply wanting to enrich or deepen existing relationships with other women, this study will lead you in a deep exploration of timeless truths in the Old and New Testaments that will help you to develop the kind of enriching and satisfying friendships that build up the body of Christ and bring honor to God.

As we dig into God's Word together week by week, we will explore these topics:

1. Why Do We Need Girlfriends and Where Do We Find Them? Understanding Our Need for Friendship with Other Women
(*Lessons from Genesis, Joshua, Judges, Ruth, 2 Samuel, Proverbs, Matthew, Luke, John*)

2. Getting Right with God: Addressing Spiritual Issues that Affect Friendship
(*Lessons from Genesis, Exodus, Deuteronomy, Joshua, 1 Kings, 2 Chronicles, Psalms, Proverbs, Isaiah, Obadiah, John, 2 Corinthians, Galatians, Ephesians, 2 Timothy, James, 1 Peter, 1 John*)

3. Clash of the Titans: Honoring God Through Relational Conflict
(*Lessons from Genesis, Leviticus, 2 Chronicles, Psalms, Proverbs, Isaiah, Matthew, Mark, John, Acts, Romans, 1 Corinthians, Ephesians, Philippians, 2 Timothy, James, 1 Peter, 1 John*)

4. The Forgiveness Business: Letting Go and Being Free
(*Lessons from Genesis, Lamentations, 1 Samuel, 2 Samuel, Psalms, Isaiah, Matthew, Luke, John, Romans, 2 Corinthians, Ephesians, Colossians, 1 Thessalonians, Hebrews, James, 1 Peter, 1 John, Revelation*)

5. Blurred Lines: Establishing Healthy Boundaries
(*Lessons from 2 Samuel, Psalms, Proverbs, Matthew, Mark, Luke, John, Romans, 1 Corinthians, 2 Corinthians, Galatians, 2 Timothy, James*)

6. Heart Sisters Do's and Don'ts: Putting It All into Practice
(*Lessons from Deuteronomy, Joshua, 1 Samuel, 2 Kings, Job, Psalms, Proverbs, Matthew, Romans, Ephesians, Philippians, 1 Thessalonians, Hebrews, James*)

By learning to cultivate God-honoring relationships, we will become more like Christ and demonstrate to a broken world His selfless, authentic love. And there's no question that our world today needs to see and know the love of Christ!

Options for Study

I love to study the Bible. I love topical studies grounded in solid, in-depth study of the Scriptures (which is my approach here), and studies of specific books of the

Bible. I love workbooks and good, old-fashioned handouts. I love DVD teachings and lessons led by an in-the-flesh Bible teacher. Just as there are a variety of spiritual gifts, there are a variety of approaches to Bible study—all originating from the same Spirit, and all having value and purpose. I also know that regardless of the Bible study we are doing with our group at a particular time, many of us will find ourselves in different seasons of life; and these seasons determine how much time we can contribute to the study. Like anything else, what you put into a study determines what you get out of it, but sometimes we can only do so much, right? Knowing this, I've designed this study so that you can make the level of commitment that best fits your current season or circumstances.

Essentially, you have three options for your participation in this study:

1. Basic Study: This includes five daily lessons for each week. Each lesson combines study of Scripture with personal reflection and application (boldface type indicates write-in-the-book questions and activities) and ends with a "Turning to God" prayer suggestion. In the margins you'll find some "Fun Facts," Scriptures, and highlights from the lessons. Before you begin each week's lessons, be sure to check out "Just Between Us" for my thoughts about the main theme we will be exploring together. Each lesson should take about twenty minutes to complete. When you gather with your group to review each week's material, you will watch a video and discuss all that you are learning.

2. Deeper Study: This level is for those who want more than just the basic study. Each week includes a memory verse, as well as several Scripture Challenges in the margins, which prompt you to dig a little deeper into the Scriptures.

3. Lighter Commitment: If the basic study feels too much for you, there is no condemnation! We've all lived through seasons in which the time we have available for study is not as much as we'd like. God will still teach you and bless you with what He wants you to know regardless of your commitment level. Offer grace to yourself!

Will you please take a moment and pray over which option is the best fit for you? When you've determined your level of participation, please fill in the circle next to each option God is nudging you to complete. Next, share your choices with someone in your group so that you will have some accountability and encouragement to keep going.

O   Prioritize group sessions. Watch the video and engage in discussion.
O   Complete as much of the homework as you can between sessions.
O   Complete all five days of homework between sessions.

O   Memorize a weekly memory verse.
O   *Complete the "Scripture Challenges" as directed.*

Encouragement Before We Begin

Perhaps you are familiar with the popular "Starfish Story." Here is my adaptation.

A man was walking along the beach one morning after a storm. He noticed a young woman standing near the shore, picking up starfish and throwing them back into the ocean. "Why are you throwing the starfish into the ocean?" the man asked. "The tide is going out, and if I do not throw them in, they will die," the young woman answered.

"But there are miles of beach and thousands of starfish. You cannot possibly make a difference!" the man replied.

The young woman listened politely, bent down to pick up another starfish, and said, "It will make a difference to this one."

The key to building up the body of Christ through authentic friendships—and influencing the watching world—is you. Like the young woman saving the starfish, we can focus on one authentic relationship at a time. And as we learn to love our friends—and others in general—we will be demonstrating the love of Christ and encouraging others to love as He loved. Before we know it, we can start a movement of loving, authentic relationships that will have a ripple effect, bringing much-needed change in a distracted and broken world. That change begins with you and me. So let's get started!

Natalie

Week 1

WHY DO WE NEED GIRLFRIENDS AND WHERE DO WE FIND THEM?

UNDERSTANDING OUR NEED FOR FRIENDSHIP WITH OTHER WOMEN

Memory Verse

Jesus replied: "'Love the Lord your God with all your heart and with all your soul and with all your mind.' This is the first and greatest commandment. And the second is like it: 'Love your neighbor as yourself.' All the Law and the Prophets hang on these two commandments."

(Matthew 22:37-40 NIV)

Just Between Us

What do you think of when you hear the phrase "Love one another"? Does it conjure up warm, fuzzy feelings, or does it slightly terrify you? It's likely a combination of both.

I have an eleven-year-old daughter and two elementary-school-aged sons. The love I feel for them is warm and fuzzy, yet it's also terrifying. Who knew you could love someone so fiercely? In full disclosure, I also have those days in which I completely understand why some species of animals eat their young. The moments of bickering over trivial details and who gets more of what is enough to make me want to wave the white flag of parenting and run away to a deserted island in the tropics.

While I know my children are good kids, I also have learned so much about the natural bent of human beings by watching them interact. Since the fall of humankind, we've struggled with what some call a "sin nature." Do you agree that we sometimes prioritize our own needs over those of others? Have you ever caught yourself trying to convince someone else to do something because it benefits you? Have you seen T-shirts for children declaring phrases such as "It's All About Me"? We can be a very self-centered lot.

But that isn't how Jesus wants us to live, and His way—the way of love—is much more difficult than it sounds. Who knew loving others could be so hard? Thankfully, God made us all wonderfully unique. He created us to have different desires, interests, opinions, and dreams. While these differences are part of what makes this world such an interesting place, they're also the reason for relational conflict; and sometimes we don't handle those conflicts with love.

Jesus is quite clear in Matthew 22: Love God above all else and love your neighbor as yourself. It really is that simple. Notice He didn't add "unless" at the end of the second commandment. He didn't say, "Love your neighbor—unless she (or he) doesn't agree with you." He didn't say, "Love your neighbor—unless she (or he) doesn't believe what you believe." Jesus said, "Love your neighbor as yourself." Period.

We have to be in relationship with other people in order to love them. According to 1 Corinthians 13:5 (NIV), love "does not dishonor others, it is not self-seeking, it is not easily angered, it keeps no record of wrongs." Does this convict you like it does me, sister? Authentic and meaningful friendships are one way we can love each other—regardless of our differences. This week we will consider why authentic friendships with other women are so important—not only to fulfill Jesus' command but also to meet some very basic needs. Friend, we were created to have Heart Sisters!

DAY 1: MADE TO RELATE

I once read somewhere that men typically feel most successful when they enjoy their occupations and are providing well for their families. On the other hand, women tend to feel most successful when their relationships are healthy and there is peace among the people in their lives. Although this is a generalization and does not apply to all, it seems to be fairly accurate according to my own observation. It really should come as no surprise to any of us who have read the creation story in Genesis. Adam was tasked with taking care of the garden while Eve was created to be in relationship with Adam. Let's take a look at the story.

Read Genesis 2:5-15 and answer the following questions.

At the beginning of the account, why had God not yet created vegetation? (vv. 5-6)

What do we learn in verse 7 that God created?

What did God create after He placed Adam in the garden? (vv. 8-9)

What did God place Adam in the garden of Eden to do? (v. 15)

Adam was created to work and care for the land. It's no wonder men tend to derive more of a sense of success from their work. This is how they were created!

Now read Genesis 2:18-25 and answer the following questions. According to verses 18 and 19, what did God observe, and how did He attempt to remedy this?

What does the second half of verse 20 tell us?

How did God create Eve? (vv. 21-22)

Eve was created from Adam because no suitable helper could be found. In other words, she was created to be in relationship with Adam because the wild animals just weren't cutting it. I believe this is why we women often feel distress when we're faced with a relational conflict or when those we love are at odds with one another. Because we were created to be in relationship with others, we can feel as if we're going to break when our relationships start to crumble.

Of course, God's purpose in creating men involves much more than work, and His purpose in creating women involves much more than being in relationship with others. In all that we do and above all else, both men and women were created to glorify God (Isaiah 43:7).

Read Genesis 10:32 in the margin. What happened after the Flood?

These are the clans of Noah's sons, according to their lines of descent, within their nations. From these the nations spread out over the earth after the flood.
(Genesis 10:32 NIV)

After the Flood, the only people who survived were Noah and his family. Noah had three sons: Shem, Ham, and Japheth. From these three sons came many offspring, and eventually it became a little too crowded for everyone to live in the same land. Therefore, the various families settled in different parts of the world so there would be enough land for them to live peacefully, as well as enough natural resources to meet the needs of the people. One specific tribe moved eastward and settled on a plain in Shinar.

Read Genesis 11:3-9. What do you learn about these people in verses 3-4? Why did God want to confuse the people who were building the tower?

If nothing were impossible for you, you would have no need for God, right? God saw that the pride among those building the tower was great. If they succeeded in their mission, they would blind themselves to the help and comfort God brings us and would be unable to glorify Him. And glorifying God—making Him known—is what God wants most for us to do.

There are many ways that we can glorify God. Yet when it comes to the ways we find fulfillment, work tends to be at the top of the list for men and relationships tend to be at the top of the list for women. This doesn't mean that women do not find fulfillment in work and men do not value relationships. It simply means that, generally speaking, we have these tendencies because that is how we were created.

We women have been supporting and encouraging one another for quite some time; this concept is nothing new. Unfortunately, we also have been competing and comparing ourselves to one another for quite some time—but we'll talk about that later in our study. Today we're going to examine a relationship between two friends in the Bible who model love and support: Elizabeth and Mary.

Read Luke 1:26-38, paying particular attention to the details that stand out to you. Try to read these verses with new eyes, and ask God to reveal truths you haven't noticed in the past. What did you notice?

Many scholars believe Mary was between twelve and fourteen years old. Now, I understand that teens back then were a little different from modern-day teens (no iPads, no social media, no phones)! Though she was a young girl who lacked in-depth knowledge of the world, she was betrothed to marry Joseph. In Jewish culture of the day, a betrothal represented a commitment almost as permanent as marriage; breaking this off would require a divorce. And did I mention she could legally be stoned to death for adultery?

Sure, she didn't commit adultery, but I think we all can agree that getting pregnant through the Holy Spirit might sound a bit outlandish to those in the community.

Mary was in need of a little comfort and truth.

Read Luke 1:39-56. Where did Mary go after she was told of the plans God had for her?

What did Elizabeth say when she saw Mary, and what happened to the baby in her womb?

What did Mary do after she heard Elizabeth's encouraging words? How do you think she may have felt?

Elizabeth's simple encouragement led Mary to compose the beautiful verses known as the Magnificat. In this song Mary glorifies God, truly accepting with peace the mission God has entrusted to her—all because of Elizabeth's encouraging words.

How has a friend encouraged you in the past?

Who is someone you can encourage today?

Fun Fact

It is believed that Elizabeth was actually a distant cousin of Mary's and was significantly older. Friendship doesn't have to be limited by location and age!

Never underestimate the power of the encouraging words you speak to the women in your life!

Never underestimate the power of the encouraging words you speak to the women in your life!

Just as Mary went straight to Elizabeth when she needed encouragement, Heart Sisters go to each other when they're feeling down and need a little pep talk. Possessing a mutual trust, they confide in each other, lift each other up by speaking truth, and help each other with the logistics of life. Elizabeth was not threatened by the fact that Mary was pregnant with the promised Messiah. Instead, she opened her home, her arms, and her heart to offer Mary comfort, encouragement, and love. Elizabeth was the ultimate Heart Sister to the mother of Jesus.

Just like Mary and Elizabeth, we all need Heart Sisters in our lives.

Turning to God

To be loved and encouraged by our friends is a great blessing; however, to find a friend who not only loves and encourages us but also helps us to walk closer with God is a rare jewel indeed. Ralph Waldo Emerson once said, "The glory of friendship is not the outstretched hand, nor the kindly smile nor the joy of companionship; it is the spiritual inspiration that comes to one when he discovers that someone else believes in him and is willing to trust him." Ask God to show you how to be this kind of friend to your friends. Make some notes in the margin if you would like to share what you've heard from God with your group.

DAY 2: NOT JUST A "WANT"

"I don't need girlfriends," she said, trying to mask the hurt I could see overtaking her pretty face. "I have my husband, and that's enough. I've been burned by women, so I just stay away," she further explained. While I understood what she was saying and could certainly identify with her feelings, I also know this leads to a very lonely existence.

I love my husband, but let's just say he doesn't always understand my thoughts and emotions because…well, he's not a woman—thankfully, of course.

A few days ago, some of my friends and I were standing around my kitchen. My husband, Jason, came home from work early and joined the conversation.

"Do you really think the grocery prices there are cheaper?" asked Jill. Jen chimed in with, "I don't know, but I like their organic selection."

"Do we really need to be eating organic or is it a hoax?" asked Rachel.

"I read online about the amount of pesticides on regular fruits and vegetables, so yes, I think so," offered Katrina. Then we started talking about how you can't always trust what you read online.

Jason was lost. He thought we were still talking about grocery prices at the store.

Now hear me out on this, sisters. I'm not saying my husband isn't a smart man, because he's brilliant (if I do say so myself). The thing is, just like a dog doesn't know what it's like to be a cat, a man doesn't know what it's like to be a woman—and vice versa.

This isn't just my opinion, either. In their renowned nurses' study, Harvard University found that women with strong networks of friends have biological as well as emotional advantages that women without these strong networks do not possess. According to the study's findings, women with strong networks of friends have lower cholesterol, lower blood pressure, and lower resting heart rates. Here's what shocked me the most: women without strong networks of friends pose the same risk to their health as smoking and being overweight.[1]

We don't just *want* friends; we *need* friends. We were created to love. Loving relationships are at the heart of the gospel. That's what we're going to unpack today.

Read Matthew 22:34-40.

What did Jesus say is the greatest commandment?

What did He say is the second-greatest commandment?

How do you think being in relationship with other women is an opportunity to love our neighbors as ourselves?

Loving God and loving others are the two basic premises of Christianity. When we choose to follow Jesus, we are choosing to love God above all else and love one another. And one of the most effective ways to love one another as we love ourselves is to engage in healthy, authentic relationships.

Yet knowing *how* to love others can be confusing and downright frustrating at times, can't it? I once saw a quote that went something like this: "I could be a Christian if it wasn't for the people." Have you ever felt that way? Loving others sounds like it should be a simple task, but let's be real: sometimes it's not. Relationships can be a difficult road to navigate, but just because we might trip along the way does not mean we should stop walking! God teaches us some of His best lessons through the bumps we stumble over.

In fact, how we handle those bumps along the way makes others stand up and take notice of our character. First Peter 2:9 says, "You are a chosen people. You are royal priests, a holy nation, God's very own possession. As a result, you can show others the goodness of God, for he called you out of the darkness into his wonderful light." Maintaining an attitude of strength and love while navigating a bumpy terrain—and even when the path is smooth—is an opportunity to show the world what we believe and why.

Read Matthew 5:13 and complete this sentence: Jesus said, "You

are the _____ of the earth."

I admit that when I first read this Scripture, I was a little confused. I can purchase a large cylinder of salt for two dollars. How valuable is that? Turns out, very. In ancient times, salt was considered extremely rare and quite valuable. Because it often was used as currency, it was the reason for a few great conflicts. The great philosopher Homer called it a "divine substance."[2] Salt was set apart. Precious.

There are more uses for salt than just seasoning our food or melting the ice on our roads. In fact, the salt industry claims fourteen thousand different uses for these small pieces of the only consumable rock in existence. Salt can be used to remove stains from clothing, brighten up the colors of vegetables, seal cracks, extinguish grease fires, and kill poison ivy to name a few.[3] Salt is not only precious and valuable. It's useful. And we're called to be "salt," which means *we* are precious, valuable, and useful.

Salt also naturally brings out the good flavor in what we eat and preserves food from spoiling; likewise, we are to bring out the good flavor in others and keep them from spoiling. In this way, we are useful to God.

Read Matthew 5:13 again, and fill in the blanks to complete the verse. (Your translation may be slightly different.)

"You are the salt of the earth. But if the salt_____

_____, how can it be made salty

again? It is _____,

except to be thrown out and trampled underfoot" (NIV).

Is it just me, or does this make you a little concerned about losing your flavor? And yes, there are days in which I feel like I've lost my flavor. There are certainly moments when I feel as if God might want to throw me out. Fortunately, God's grace covers those less than favorable moments, and the truth is, He will *never* throw us out!

Now let's read Matthew 5:14-16. What else does Jesus say we are? And what are we supposed to do?

Not only are we called to be salt—which means to be set apart, precious, valuable, and useful—but we're also called to be light.

Like salt, there is a certain power in light, which we often take for granted. Light allows us to function after the sun goes down. It makes scary moments feel not as frightening. It produces a comforting glow. Figuratively, light illuminates the secrets we want to keep in the darkness, so that they lose their power over us. Light is even more powerful, illuminating darkness, reducing fear, and encouraging truth. But what happens when our light is hidden?

Sometimes people can see a joy in others, and it threatens them. For example, one of my friends is having a tough time being "set apart" among her long-time group of friends because she's a new follower of Jesus and her friends are not. She dims her light by downplaying her faith, not living a life that is obviously set apart, because she doesn't want to be different or seen as self-righteous—and I completely understand because I've been in that situation before. However, if we continue doing what we've always done, how will anyone know we are different and set apart? That doesn't mean we should be self-righteous and act as if we're "holier than thou," but

Dimming our light for the sake of belonging ultimately results in an extinguished flame.

it does mean we have a responsibility to show the world we know Jesus by being bold and unashamed in our faith. Dimming our light for the sake of belonging ultimately results in an extinguished flame.

What are some ways you may be dimming your light? Check all that apply:

_____ **Spending time with people who don't make you feel good about who God created you to be.**

_____ **Believing lies about who the world says you are ("You're too much" or "You're not enough").**

_____ **Not speaking up when others are speaking negatively about someone else.**

_____ **Refusing to surrender pride because you want everyone to believe you have it all figured out.**

_____ **Using words to tear down rather than build up (gossiping, speaking ill of others, criticizing, etc.).**

_____ **Comparing yourself to others and being envious of what you don't have.**

_____ **Fearing rejection, failure, or judgment.**

_____ **Forgetting you've been forgiven and redeemed.**

Salt and light. It's a bit of a tall order, sisters. We're called to be set apart, precious, valuable, useful, powerful, illuminating, fear-reducing, and truth-seeking—in *all* of our relationships. Now, if that isn't a definition of love, I don't know what is! But the best news of all is that we are not on our own; we have Christ within us, and He is the Light of the world! Shining our light and being salt—or set apart—is exactly what we're called to do.

Daniel 12:3 says, "Those who are wise will shine like the brightness of the heavens, and those who lead many to righteousness, like the stars for ever and ever" (NIV). Let's be wise and shine brightly, sisters! Let's love our friends well by showing them the authentic light of Jesus.

Turning to God

Spend some time with God surrendering the stuff that dims your light. Ask Him to search your heart and reveal things you've never even realized were dimming your light, and then surrender those as well. On the lightbulb on the next page, write at least two ways you will shine for God this week. Examples could be striving to not speak negative thoughts or to see the brokenness of those who hurt you instead of immediately getting angry and defensive.

DAY 3: SEEK AND YOU WILL FIND

Once upon a time, I thought I had to be best friends with everyone I came into contact with on any given day. From casual acquaintances to my closest friends, I mistakenly believed I was supposed to invest in all of those relationships. What I didn't quite understand at the time is that we all have just twenty-four hours each day. Figure in time to sleep, time to eat, time to do laundry (can I get an amen?), time to care for children, and time to work (whether you work outside of the home or not, you still work) and you're down to precious few hours. I ran myself ragged in an attempt to be there for everyone, and eventually it was the ones I love the most who suffered the most: my sweet family.

When you find yourself doing ministry and forgetting your first ministry, you've gotten it twisted, sister, and I was indeed one twisted sister.

Fun Fact

Mary was the woman who poured the expensive oil on Jesus' feet just days before He was crucified (John 12:1-8). Pure nard was a powerful and aromatic oil, and experts believe it still would have been fragrant at the time of Jesus' death.

What I didn't know then but, thankfully, do now is that we can't be best friends with everyone. There simply aren't enough hours in the day. Within our Heart Sister relationships, there are three categories or levels: (1) Inner Heart Friends (our very closest friends), (2) Middle Heart Friends (close friends), and (3) Outer Heart Friends (good friends). The outer perimeter is labeled as "Heart Potential" because it's important to always keep our hearts open to new friendships.

Let's look at these three categories through the lens of the relationships of Someone we all know and love: Jesus.

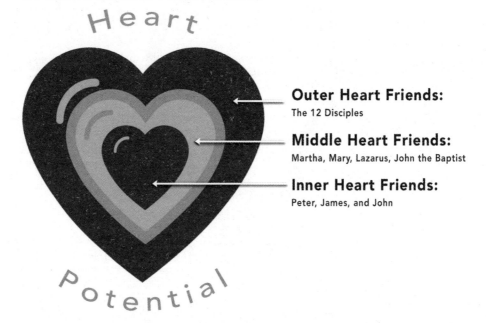

Outer Heart Friends:
The 12 Disciples

Middle Heart Friends:
Martha, Mary, Lazarus, John the Baptist

Inner Heart Friends:
Peter, James, and John

Read Matthew 16:27-28 (NIV) and complete the verses below. (Your translation may be different.)

²⁷ *"For the Son of Man _____ in his Father's glory with his angels, and then he will reward each person according to what they have done."*

²⁸ *"Truly I tell you, _____*

_____ will not taste death before they see the Son of Man coming in his kingdom."

Jesus was speaking to the disciples about when He will eventually return to the earth. He then mentioned there were some among this group of disciples who would not have to wait until they died to see the glory of Jesus and the angels. As we learn in the next chapter of Matthew, Jesus would choose a few of his disciples to witness a special moment in which His glory would be revealed.

Have you ever been chosen for something, such as a promotion at work or an award? Have you ever been a young person's chosen favorite? Have you ever been selected to participate in a special panel or discussion? If so, how did you feel to be chosen?

If not, what do you think it would feel like to be chosen? (And guess what? You *are* chosen—by God!)

Read Matthew 17:1-13. Why do you think the Transfiguration was a special and intimate time for Jesus?

Which of His disciples did Jesus choose to join him on the mountain? Write their names below:

1.

2.

3.

Jesus chose Peter, James, and John to accompany Him to the mountain so that they could witness the moment of truth: Jesus' appearance literally changed into that of His heavenly glory. In fact, the Greek word *metemorphōthē* is used in Matthew 17:2 and means "an alteration in form"

Fun Fact

Peter was the friend Jesus tasked with starting the early church (Matthew 16:18). John was the disciple Jesus loved and entrusted to care for his mother, Mary, after His death (19:26). James was John's brother, who was the first apostle to die for his faith (Acts 12:2).

Fun Fact

James and John were nicknamed the "Sons of Thunder" by Jesus (Mark 3:17) because of their boisterous and sometimes fiery tempers. John later became known as the "Apostle of Love" because he preached so often about loving each other.[5] He started his relationship with Jesus as a "Son of Thunder," and after many years of following Him, he became known for love. John was transformed through his relationship with Jesus, and we all are given this same opportunity!

or "to change outwardly and physically."[4] Jesus trusted Peter, James, and John enough to reveal His true self, which proved He was who He said He was. He then asked them to keep it quiet.

Why did Jesus want to keep something so wonderful a secret? Jesus was strategic about what He revealed about Himself and to whom. Early in His ministry, He wanted others to hear His message more than He wanted them to be impressed with His healing abilities and divine nature. Yet Jesus wanted His closest friends to see Him for who He really was. Peter, James, and John were His closest friends—those He trusted completely. They were what I call Inner Heart Friends.

Jesus also had Middle Heart Friends. Middle Heart Friends are still close friends—they're just not as intimate as Inner Heart Friends. Lazarus, Mary, and Martha are examples of Jesus' Middle Heart Friends.

> **Read Luke 10:38-42; John 11:1-44; 12:1-8. Based on these accounts, how do we know Jesus was close to Lazarus, Mary, and Martha?**

> **Do you most identify with Lazarus, Mary, or Martha? Why?**

> **What is something you can learn from this person's relationship with Jesus?**

Finally, the remaining nine disciples (minus John, James, and Peter) were Jesus' Outer Heart Friends. Sure, He loved, trusted, and valued them as friends; however, in comparison to those individuals I have labeled His Middle and Inner Heart Friends (a comparison I am making based upon what I read in Scripture about those relationships), the other disciples' relationship with Jesus does not appear to have been as close or intimate. However, no doubt as He spent time with them during his three-year ministry, teaching them and traveling with them, they developed a very strong bond.

Understanding these three categories of friendships gives us such freedom and grace. Once I was talking to a woman who said, "I don't have time for any more friends, so I don't really try to get to know anyone else." Truthfully, I get it. As I mentioned earlier, we can't be best friends with everyone because we have only so many hours in the day. Yet at the same time, we need to keep our hearts open to new relationships. If we fail to do so, we might deprive ourselves of some very meaningful friendships! We reach our full "Heart Potential" when we keep our hearts open to new relationships while allowing ourselves the freedom to have Outer, Middle, and Inner Heart Friends.

As someone who moved to a new community eight years ago, I'm so thankful my friends kept an open heart toward the new people they met, because I was one of those new people! Now I try to keep my heart open toward others, welcoming any new friendships that God might have planned for me. Whether we're actively seeking new friendships or feeling content with the relationships we already have, the truth is that God always wants us to keep an open heart.

Turning to God

As a recovering people pleaser, I've had to accept the reality that I can't be everything to everyone, nor can I be best friends with everyone. The truth is, all that people-pleasing, wanting-to-be-best-friends-with-everyone stuff—it's rooted in pride. Yes, ma'am. Pride. Ick.

When we try to please everyone, we're trying to be everyone's everything. However, there's one small problem: only Jesus can be our everything. So when I try to be everything to everyone, I'm putting myself on level ground with Jesus.

Today, turn to God and tell Him you want Him to be your everything. Confess if you, like me, have tried to be everything to everyone, and release those you love into His care. Rest in your freedom, and let God do what God knows how to do.

DAY 4: IT TAKES ALL KINDS, PART 1

When my daughter turned four, she was completely into cheerleading. She wore a red and white cheerleading uniform every single day without fail. (I should probably also note there was no way to clean said uniform because of all the sequins and glitter.) If anyone asked her what she

Whether we're actively seeking new friendships or feeling content with the relationships we already have, the truth is that God always wants us to keep an open heart.

wanted to be when she grew up, she quickly responded with "a professional cheerleader." Naturally, I didn't even have to ask her what kind of birthday cake she wanted.

At the urging of a few friends who claimed it was easy to make simple, cute birthday cakes, I decided I could probably handle it. I Googled "cheerleading cakes" and found a megaphone cake that could be made with a 9 × 13 pan and a donut as a handle.

Except my version didn't turn out so cute, and it certainly wasn't easy.

It would have been easy for my friend Laurie, because she's a gifted cake and cookie decorator and knows what she's doing. Me, on the other hand? Not so much. I now have no shame in purchasing my children's birthday cakes because it's better for us all. Cake decorating is not my thing!

We are all different with unique gifts, but there is at least one way we're the same: *we all need each other.*

As iron sharpens iron, so one person sharpens another.
(Proverbs 27:17 NIV)

Read Proverbs 27:17 in the margin. What do we learn from this verse?

We were all created with unique personalities that shape our perspectives and opinions. Just as the sharpening of one iron blade against another makes it more effective, close friends help sharpen our character and make us more effective. But what kinds of friends should we seek if we want to ensure we'll be encouraged to grow in our faith?

Today and tomorrow we are going to learn about seven women of the Bible who represent the different types of friends we want to have with us on our faith journey: Rahab, Deborah, Bathsheba, Ruth, Naomi, Mary, and Elizabeth. I call them the "Super Seven Sisters." We'll examine different aspects of their personalities and what we can learn from each, and you can decide which one you identify with most. What kind of friend are you to others? What kinds of friends do you have? The "Super Seven Sisters" will help you identify just that.

While having a group of "Super Seven Sisters" is a goal we can work toward, there are no hard-and-fast rules here. Maybe your Martha friend is also your Mary friend. The quality of our friendships is more important than the quantity of friends we have. On the other hand, while you may not have seven close friends, it's less than ideal to have just one girlfriend because she cannot be your everything. That could put too much pressure on her shoulders, and your friendship could suffer.

It's also possible to have a whole host of friends but none who walk closely with you—in sync with your heart. I've been in this situation before, and it's a lonely place to be. Though you may be surrounded by people often, having too many "surface" friendships can cause you to feel unheard, increase your desire to be known, and make you feel that something is missing in your relationships—you just might not know what that something is. Perhaps author Kim Culbertson said it best in her book *The Liberation of Max McTrue*: "People think being alone makes you lonely but I don't think that's true. Being surrounded by the wrong people is the loneliest thing in the world."[6]

Surrounding yourself with the right people can literally change your life. So let's take a look at our "Super Seven Sisters," beginning with the first three.

1. Rahab

Read Joshua 2 and write four words you would use to describe Rahab. Then put a star by the quality you admire the most.

1.

2.

3.

4.

Why do you admire this quality?

Now read Joshua 6:22-25. What happened as a result of Rahab's courage?

During the time of Rahab's story, Jericho was known as a corrupt city in the land of Canaan filled with idol worshipers. God had promised to one day give the land back to the Israelites when the "sin of the Amorites" reached its "full measure" (Genesis 15:16 NIV). The Amorites were descended from the sons of Canaan. Apparently, Jericho had reached its full measure of sin! Whether or not Rahab possessed the wisdom to see that the two spies were on a mission from God that ultimately would achieve a greater good by delivering the Israelites back to the land they were once promised, she knew that the Lord had given them the land and that He was the God of heaven and earth (Joshua 2:8-11). So she chose to hide the spies, which resulted in her entire family being spared.

A "Rahab friend" is bold and courageous. She will speak for you when you can't, and she will lovingly speak God's truth if you aren't living your life for God. She is willing to speak and act on truth while keeping your best interest a top priority—which is exactly what Rahab did, isn't it? I like to think that Rahab was able to see the big picture, the greater good of defending the Israelites. Whether she had faith in their mission or simply reverent fear of their God, she possessed a stoic courage I so admire.

We need courage in today's world, don't you think? This is precisely why our Rahab friends are so important; we need women who are courageous enough to speak and act on the truth in love!

2. Deborah

Read Judges 4:1-3. After the death of Ehud, what happened to the Israelites?

During the period of the judges, the people were not yet united under one king. It was a time of extreme oppression for the Israelites, and Deborah proved to be a fearless and bold leader. Each tribe lived independently, and people who lived near these tribes sometimes took advantage of their vulnerability. Several tribes together would be too strong to attempt an attack; however, individual tribes were more susceptible to attack. During Deborah's time, the Canaanite king Jabin of Hazor mercilessly oppressed the Jews, along with a brutal general named Sisera. Deborah remained true to God during this time, and the people flocked to her to hear words of wisdom and encouragement. Ultimately she came up with a plan to defeat the Canaanites.

Throughout their history, the Israelites had cycles of faithful obedience where they really seemed to understand God and how He works, followed by cycles of extreme despair and foolishness—sort of like me. Maybe you can relate, too. Regardless, this was a period of intense hardship for the Israelites.

Now read Judges 4:4-9. Is there something about Deborah or this glimpse of her story that resonates with you? If so, why?

I'm guessing you discovered that a "Deborah friend" is bold, courageous, wise, and possesses strong leadership skills. When a crisis strikes, she will remain levelheaded and calm. She's also the first friend you'll seek when you're in need of wise counsel.

C. S. Lewis once said, "The next best thing to being wise oneself is to live in a circle of those who are."[7] When we can't know everything (and who can?), a Deborah friend can help.

3. Bathsheba

Read 2 Samuel 11. We don't know much about Bathsheba's character at this point, but we do know she has experienced some challenging times. On the line below, create a timeline of the events described in 2 Samuel 11. The first and last have been added for you.

David's troops go to war, but David remains in Jerusalem.

Bathsheba gives birth to a son.

I've always had a soft heart toward Bathsheba. During this period of time, if she had refused to go to King David—well, let's just say Uriah likely would have returned home to find a dead wife. Women didn't have many rights at that time, and most certainly, if the king summoned you, you weren't given much choice in the matter. Bathsheba wasn't being passive; she was being prudent.

Read 2 Samuel 12:15-24. What was the consequence of David's sin? How do you think this impacted Bathsheba?

Fun Fact

Deborah was a prophetess—someone who spoke for God. There are ten identified female prophets in the Bible, showing that God values and loves His daughters and will speak through them regardless of gender!

Scripture Challenge

Take a look at 1 Kings 1:1-31 to find out what bold action Bathsheba took years later on behalf of her son, Solomon.

> **I'm certain God intends to mold us and make us more like his Son through our relationships.**

How did the Lord show them grace?

How would you describe Bathsheba's character after reading these passages?

Bathsheba walked through some trials, wouldn't you say? She's often portrayed as an adulteress, but again, she didn't have much of a choice in the matter. When the king summoned, you went—no questions asked! She lived through her husband's death and the death of a child—two unfathomable losses. Yet through both of those tragedies, she remained loyal, steadfast, and committed to the son she later conceived, Solomon.

In 1 Kings 1:15 we see further evidence of Bathsheba's courage and persistence through her insistence that a dying King David carry out his promise of crowning Solomon as the new king. Another of David's sons, Adonijah, had manipulated his way to the throne even though it had been promised to Solomon, and Bathsheba was having none of that! Hell hath no fury like a mama whose child has been scorned!

Bathsheba friends have walked through trials and lived to tell about them. In fact, it's their trials that have made them courageous, compassionate, and calm.

I love how God has created each of us to be so wonderfully unique. If we were all the same, no one would ever learn and grow, and the world would be such a boring place! I'm also so thankful for the array of personalities my Heart Sisters possess, because their differences offer unparalleled perspectives and insights I otherwise would not have uncovered. I believe the people in our lives are no accident. I'm certain God intends to mold us and make us more like his Son through our relationships. The diversity of our Heart Sisters is one way He does just that.

Turning to God

Rahab, Deborah, and Bathsheba possessed traits that are pleasing to God—traits we can strive to develop in ourselves.

Which of the traits we discussed today would you like to develop further in yourself? Write it below:

Talk to God about what is stopping you from developing this trait and the help you need from God. For example, if you would like to develop more courage but fear is stopping you, talk to God about what you are afraid of and ask Him to give you the strength you need.

Record your thoughts in the space below. Then read the definition of a breath prayer in the margin, and create a short breath prayer that you can recite whenever you need help with your desired trait.

Fun Fact

A breath prayer is a spiritual tool that can help you to center your thoughts on God and God's ever-present help. Choose a short phrase or Scripture prayer, saying the first part as you inhale and the second part as you exhale. For example, "Lord Jesus, be my strength."

DAY 5: IT TAKES ALL KINDS, PART 2

When I was in high school, there was a group of girls who wanted to cut off my hair. I'm not kidding.

At the start of my freshman year, there were three girls who became the targets for the older girls' bullying. I was the lucky winner of one of those not-so-coveted spots. In between classes, I would rush to my locker, heart racing and palms sweaty, to retrieve my books for the next class and get on my merry way as fast as possible. I wish I were kidding when I tell you there were four girls who followed me during passing periods with long shears, walking intimidatingly behind my back as they opened and closed those sharp blades.

I was terrified.

After this had been happening for a few weeks, my friends Holly and Jennifer committed to show up at my locker in between classes to ensure I was safe and to calm my frazzled, steeped-in-fear nerves. And you know what? Their love, support, and loyalty were just the balm I needed to see this was a comma in my story, not a period. Commas tell readers to pause for a moment; the commas in our lives are pauses in which times might be hard, but the story isn't finished yet.

I can't help thinking of Holly and Jennifer when I think of Ruth—number four of our "Super Seven Sisters." Let's continue our exploration of these women who represent the different types of friends we want to have with us on our faith journey. Because Ruth and Naomi's lives were intertwined, we will read their story through once and then revisit verses as we consider their traits separately.

4. Ruth

Read all of Ruth 1. Then reread verses 16 through 19. What one word would you use to describe Ruth?

How does (or would) it make you feel to know you have someone who is unfalteringly loyal to you?

I can't even begin to grasp the magnitude of Ruth's utter and complete unselfishness. After all, she was still young and could easily find a husband. She wasn't necessarily responsible for her mother-in-law. And it would be much more difficult to find a new husband with her mother-in-law in tow. There were many reasons why Ruth should have just cut her losses and moved on. Yet that is not what she did. Ruth chose the more difficult option because she was loyal and committed to honoring her mother-in-law.

A few years ago, our family had a conflict with another family that lived in our neighborhood. The situation was handled poorly on both sides, and the conflict still remains unresolved—much to my dismay. Another friend of mine shot down any rumors or unflattering comments that were made about our family because she knew the truth of what happened. This friend is a "Ruth friend"—loyal, unwavering, and committed to truth.

5. Naomi

Reread Ruth 1:8-9. What one word would you use to describe Naomi?

When I read the Book of Ruth, I am struck by Naomi's utter and complete selflessness. During biblical times, if you were a widow, your sons took care of you. However, both of Naomi's sons died, so she literally had no one. It's tempting to see this situation through our own eyes as women living in the twenty-first century and assume she could care for herself. Why couldn't she just get a job? Why couldn't she go to the bank and get a loan or draw from savings, if she had any?

That's not how it was during the times of Ruth and Naomi. Women didn't have the same rights, and their voices generally were not heard. They were considered second-class citizens, which means it would have been very difficult for her to earn a living. She also was too old to remarry. Naomi likely would have ended up as a beggar on the streets.

For Naomi to urge her daughters-in-law to go back to their family homes and find new husbands was the ultimate act of selflessness, wasn't it? Because Naomi loved Ruth and Orpah, she wanted what was best for them—even though it meant an uncertain and bleak future for herself.

Reread Ruth 1:12. What did Naomi call her daughters-in-law? Why do you think she called them this?

Naomi had an intense love for these women who married her sons. Why do you think Naomi loved Orpah and Ruth so much?

Why do you think showing kindness is so powerful?

To whom can you show kindness today?

A "Naomi friend" is loving and unselfish. She makes a great mentor because she likely has had more life experience than you've had, and she can offer insight, wisdom, and truth.

Has a friend ever done something for you because it was what was best for you—even though she didn't benefit? If your mind is drawing a blank, I would encourage you to spend some time talking to God about this. Ask Him to reveal a time when you've been loved so selflessly by someone who was willing to lay down her needs for your own. Write—or draw—your thoughts below.

May I issue you a challenge for today? Whoever came to your mind, take a moment to handwrite a note to that person (no e-mail, text, or phone call!), thanking her for her selflessness and love.

When my grandmother passed away years ago, I found a manila envelope of sweet notes she received from those she loved. I remember her telling me she would pull them out on the hard days. You know the ones: those days when you forget who you are and whose you are. The days when you believe the lies the world tells you. The days when you think you just can't do it anymore. I don't think we can ever fully understand the power of our handwritten words to those we love. They have the power to change the trajectory of our days and transform our hearts.

Take a moment today to encourage the one who loved you so well. Who knows? Maybe your note will end up in her envelope of encouragement!

6. Mary

Ruth and Naomi weren't the only loyal and steadfast women in the Bible. Mary, the mother of Jesus, possessed so many redeeming qualities that it's difficult to list them all!

Read Luke 1:26-38; 2:16-19; and John 19:25-26. Based on these accounts, how would you describe Mary?

These Scriptures make Mary more human to me. As the mother of Jesus, Mary is rightfully exalted, revered, and respected. But we tend to put her on a pedestal and forget she was a young girl who eventually became a woman with a heart for her son, just like any other mother.

In Luke 2, we see that the word about the birth of the Messiah is quickly spreading, and Mary knows it. Before more visitors arrive and the pressure of mothering the Messiah sets in, including having to share her son with so many, we see that Mary "treasured up all these things and pondered them in her heart" (v. 19 NIV). She treasured this quiet moment with her infant son so she could recall it later when the challenges came.

As a mother myself, I have mental snapshots of my children's faces at younger ages frozen in my memory. When they're adults, I know I will still see those faces. Like Mary, I treasure these things in my heart, too. I can relate to this Mary.

A "Mary friend" is a trustworthy prayer warrior. She's steadfast and loving and has a strong desire to live a life pleasing to God. Even if you don't communicate with her regularly, you know she's always there for you, and you can pick up right where you left off.

7. Elizabeth

We talked about the relationship between Mary and Elizabeth on Day 1, but now let's look at Elizabeth and then reexamine her friendship with Mary through the lens of qualities we look for in a friend.

Read Luke 1:1-25. What do we know about Elizabeth from verses 5 and 7?

How did her husband, Zechariah, react to the angel's news of her pregnancy, and what happened to him as a result? (vv. 18, 20)

How was Elizabeth's reaction to this news different from her husband's reaction? (v. 25) What can we conclude about Elizabeth based on this?

Reread Luke 1:39-45, which we read on Day 1. How else would you describe Elizabeth?

Elizabeth was a faithful woman who possessed the gift of encouragement. However, before we label her as a quiet and timid little mouse, let's read another part of her story.

Read Luke 1:57-65. What do these verses further reveal about Elizabeth?

Elizabeth was actually quite bold, wasn't she? Remember that during this time in history, women didn't speak up very often. Now, of course, Elizabeth probably had to do a little more speaking up since her husband, Zechariah, was unable to talk, but she still defied the cultural expectation to honor God's instructions. Not only are "Elizabeth friends" gifted encouragers but they also are committed to honoring and pleasing God.

Ruth, Naomi, Mary, and Elizabeth possessed traits that please God and help others to grow in their faith—traits we can strive to develop in ourselves.

Which of the traits we discussed today would you like to develop further in yourself? Write it below:

Now, let's have some fun. For each of the "Super Seven Women," write the names of people you know who fit that description.

1. Rahab—bold, courageous
A Rahab friend will lovingly speak truth if you aren't living your life for God.

2. Deborah—strong leader, wise
A Deborah friend remains calm when a crisis strikes. She also offers a wise, biblical perspective when advice is needed.

3. Bathsheba—tough with just the right balance of grace and truth
A Bathsheba friend has been through tough times and lived to tell about them. She'll walk through adversity with you and reassure you that good will come out of life's struggles.

4. Ruth—loyal and true
A Ruth friend is faithful and always on your side—no matter what!

5. Naomi—selfless, loving, older
A Naomi friend is older than you and can serve as your spiritual mentor.

6. Mary—trustworthy, prayer warrior
Even when you are not able to connect as often as you would like, a Mary friend is someone with whom you can always pick up right where you left off.

7. Elizabeth—encourager, bold and obedient
An Elizabeth friend is an earthly encourager who helps keep you going! She builds you up with pep talks and always points you back to truth.

Now put a star beside the woman who sounds the most like *you*!

Not only do our friends have different personality types, as represented by the "Super Seven Sisters" we've examined, they also fall into different categories or groups. I've observed that most of us seem to have at least five different categories of friends. This doesn't mean we have all five of these categories of friends, so don't feel like you're lacking if you don't! It just means that in this culture of social media and technology, relationships have evolved, making our connectivity far greater than it once was—for better or for worse!

(1) *Online friends* are people you might not know in real life but to whom you feel deeply connected. In our digital world, meeting friends through social media groups, blogs, and online book studies is not uncommon. **(2)** *Real-life friends* are the ones who will be there when you've been in bed with the flu for days and someone needs to feed your family. They're the ones you meet for lunch and leave feeling refreshed and refueled. (Having online friends without real-life friends can feel very lonely.) **(3)** *Narrow path friends* are followers of Jesus who help to keep us on the narrow path that leads to God and discourages us from choosing the wide path the world offers. **(4)** *Mentor/mentee friends* are those who are mentoring us and those whom we are mentoring. **(5)** *Ministry/work friends* are the friends we know from working together in some capacity.

List some of your friends in these categories:

1. Online friends

2. Real-life friends

3. Narrow path friends

4. Mentor/mentee friends

5. Ministry/work friends

Do you think it is important to have friends in each of these categories? Why or why not?

With all this talk about types and categories of friends, I'd like to end our week of study with an important word about cliques and tight-knit groups of friends. You see, there's a critical distinction between the two. Allow me to explain.

Cliques can indeed be very hurtful. I know this from experience, and I suspect you do, too. Is there anyone who has never felt excluded by a clique at some point? I doubt it. Yet sometimes we can be turned off by what we think is a clique of women but actually is a tight-knit group of friends. The difference is in how they welcome you.

A clique will make you feel less than. Sure, they might say hello during introductions, but that's about it, my friend. They won't ask you many questions about yourself, and they won't make any attempt to include you. On the other hand, a tight-knit group of friends might appear to be a clique to an outsider because they're close and they know one another well; however, they welcome new people by asking them questions about themselves, they work hard to make you feel welcome and included, and they will include you in plans they're making while together. It's important to recognize the difference between cliques and tight-knit groups of friends because incorrectly labeling a group of women as a clique might deprive you of some very dear Heart Sisters!

As we close today, I would like to remind us why we need Heart Sisters: to love one another. One way to love our neighbors as ourselves is to be in relationship with other people—but we can't be in relationship with other people if we isolate ourselves because of our own fear. God has made it clear that we were created to be in relationship. He has blessed us with women in our lives who possess different personalities, strengths, and weaknesses, and He has provided various avenues to connect with these women. Having authentic friendships is a symbiotic relationship—in other words, both parties benefit. God has known this from the beginning. So when we cultivate Heart Sisters in our lives, we are fulfilling God's plan for us. Yet another reason to be thankful for God and His all-knowing provision!

Scripture Challenge

The Hebrew word *goel*, used to designate the kinsman-redeemer in the Bible, means one who delivers, rescues, or redeems property or people. In the story of Ruth, the kinsman-redeemer is Boaz. To find further examples of kinsman-redeemers, read Leviticus 25:25-28; Deuteronomy 25:5-10; Ruth 3:1-4; and Matthew 22:23-28. Next, read Isaiah 43:1-7, which shows that God is our kinsman-redeemer who redeems us through the blood of His Son, Jesus Christ.

Turning to God

Wow, we've covered quite a bit this week, haven't we? My prayer is that you have a deeper understanding of why we need female friends, appreciate the importance of having different kinds of friends, and feel hopeful—and expectant—about having close girlfriends.

What is your main takeaway from this week of study? Spend some time asking God what He has for you, and then write or draw your thoughts below.

WHY DO WE NEED GIRLFRIENDS AND WHERE DO WE FIND THEM?

We were _____ for relationship.

ezer kenegdo – a helper of the same nature as God, providing strength and protection

God intends for us to have_____ _____.

Mary Visits Elizabeth

³⁹ At that time Mary got ready and hurried to a town in the hill country of Judea, ⁴⁰ where she entered Zechariah's home and greeted Elizabeth. ⁴¹ When Elizabeth heard Mary's greeting, the baby leaped in her womb, and Elizabeth was filled with the Holy Spirit. ⁴² In a loud voice she exclaimed: "Blessed are you among women, and blessed is the child you will bear! ⁴³ But why am I so favored, that the mother of my Lord should come to me? ⁴⁴ As soon as the sound of your greeting reached my ears, the baby in my womb leaped for joy. ⁴⁵ Blessed is she who has believed that the Lord would fulfill his promises to her!"

(Luke 1:39-45 NIV)

We _____ other women.

VIDEO VIEWER GUIDE: WEEK 1

The Two Greatest Commandments

37 Jesus replied: "'Love the Lord your God with all your heart and with all your soul and with all your mind.' 38 This is the first and greatest commandment. 39 And the second is like it: 'Love your neighbor as yourself.'

(Matthew 22:37-39 NIV)

_____ with other _____ is an opportunity to

live out Jesus' commandment to love others.

Week 2

GETTING RIGHT WITH GOD

ADDRESSING SPIRITUAL ISSUES
THAT AFFECT FRIENDSHIP

Memory Verse

"If my own people will humbly pray and turn back to me and stop sinning, then I will answer them from heaven. I will forgive them."

(2 Chronicles 7:14 CEV)

Just Between Us

My family is in the process of moving to a new home, and we are in a temporary residence for the next six months. Can I be straight with you? I despise moving; it can bring out the worst in human behavior—specifically, my own.

Some of our belongings currently are in storage, and the monthly cost of a storage unit along with apartment rent happens to be more expensive than our prior mortgage—which has left our budget more than a little tight. As a result, we are not traveling this summer.

I know what a first-world issue that is! I am *insanely blessed*—much more than I deserve. Yet when I see the photos that my friends are posting on social media of their fun family vacations, I admit that I feel a little envious. Such an ugly part of my soul I'm revealing here!

Last week, one of my Heart Sisters returned from vacation and wanted to tell me all about it. Now, I usually want to hear these details. I love my Heart Sisters! They really are my *sisters*. But this time, I felt a twinge of discontent, which led to a less-than-enthusiastic response to my friend. Yuck. I hate to even write these words, friend.

A few days later, I realized that my unenthusiastic response might have confused and hurt my friend. God had been working on my heart (mortar and pestle style, if you know what I mean!) and had revealed my sin in the situation. I confessed and sought His forgiveness, and then I did the same with my friend.

Here's the thing, sister. If I had been in a good place with God, then my first response would have been to rejoice with my friend rather than feel sorry for myself. If I had been living in the fullness of God's Spirit that day, I would have been content. Of course, we are human and often miss the mark (sin), but as followers of Jesus we are called to strive to fill ourselves with the goodness He provides—not the "goodness" the world provides.

This week we'll be talking about the "junk" (sin) that negatively impacts our relationships. I've observed that when we do not have a right relationship with God, we do not have a right relationship with others. Our relationship with the Lord is the thermostat that sets the temperature of how we relate to others. We'll not only talk about the junk that negatively impacts our relationships but we'll also discuss how to get right with God—which enables us to get right with others. A stronger relationship with God is the gateway to stronger relationships with other people—and who doesn't want stronger relationships with God and others?

DAY 1: JOY-STEALING COMPARISON

Years ago, before I became a follower of Jesus, I searched in vain for something that would fill the God-shaped hole in my life. Boyfriends. Pretty clothes. Status. Performance. My physical appearance. In other words, I sought things of the world to satisfy my deepest longing—my innate desire to be in relationship with God.

This innate desire isn't just something God placed in my heart. He has placed the same desire in yours as well. However, sometimes we don't quite understand that it's not a "what" we desire but a "who" we desire: God. Until we seek God and begin a relationship with Him, we will always be longing for something—though we may not always know what that longing is.

[19] We love each other because he loved us first. [20] If someone says, "I love God," but hates a fellow believer, that person is a liar; for if we don't love people we can see, how can we love God, whom we cannot see?

(1 John 4:19-20)

Read 1 John 4:19-20 in the margin, and then summarize the verses in your own words inside the heart below.

God wants to be in relationship with us. Yet even after we choose to love God, we still struggle with sin. Wouldn't it be great if we were fully sanctified—conformed into the image of Jesus—as soon as we accept Him as our Lord and Savior? But the reality is that sanctification is a lifelong process, and our struggle against sin continues as long as we live in this broken world. Our sin separates us from God, weakening our relationship with Him. Just like an argument separates us for a time from our earthly family, sin separates us from our Heavenly Father.

During the next five days, we will be discussing five common sins that affect us as women and how they separate us from God. Getting right with God is the first step in cultivating authentic relationships, because it's hard to keep our relationships in sync when our relationship with God is out of sync. In fact, it's impossible. The other relationships in our lives are not going to be healthy until our relationship with the Lord is healthy. Let's start with one relationship barrier that I'm certain we're all familiar with: comparison.

Read Genesis 29:1-13. Who are the three main people in this passage?

1.

2.

3.

Now read Genesis 29:14-29. Whom do we meet in these verses, and what happens?

Talk about family drama! Jacob fell in love with Rachel and worked for Laban for seven years to earn the right to marry Laban's daughter. Yet on the night of their marriage, he was duped into marrying Rachel's older sister, Leah—because it was customary for the oldest to marry first. Laban was completely deceitful, tricking Jacob into marrying his less desirable daughter. As unfortunate as that was, I feel the most sorry for Leah, because suddenly she found herself married to a man who didn't choose her, want her, or love her.

Scripture Challenge

Check out the following Scriptures for more insight into God's desire to be in relationship with us: Leviticus 26:12; Proverbs 8:17; John 15:12-17; Acts 17:27; 1 John 3:1-2; 4:19.

Comparison happens when we are looking sideways at what others have instead of looking up to what God has for us.

Reread Genesis 29:16-17, 30. What do you learn about Leah and Rachel in these verses? How would you feel if you were Leah?

After Jacob and Leah's bridal week was complete, Jacob was allowed to marry Rachel, but he had to promise to work for Laban another seven years. Interestingly enough, though Jacob loved Rachel and preferred her over Leah, he soon grew to care for Leah greatly—probably because she bore him so many sons. But we're getting ahead of ourselves; we'll talk more about that tomorrow. For now, these verses set the stage for Leah and Rachel's upcoming comparison battle.

Here's the thing about comparison: it breathes death and steals joy. Comparison happens when we are looking sideways at what others have instead of looking up to what God has for us.

Read Galatians 6:3-5 in the margin. What are we responsible for according to verse 5?

3 If anyone thinks they are something when they are not, they deceive themselves. 4 Each one should test their own actions. Then they can take pride in themselves alone, without comparing themselves to someone else, 5 for each one should carry their own load.
(Galatians 6:3-5 NIV)

God asks us simply to carry our own load, not someone else's load. Isn't that the best news ever? Comparing ourselves to others in any way is both unnecessary and unhelpful.

While the word *load* in verse 5 refers to our individual burdens, we need to remember that we also carry individual "blessings" or gifts. I might desire to lead worship, create beautiful quilts, or decorate amazing birthday cakes, but those are not blessings God has chosen to bestow upon me. Likewise, others may desire the blessings God has given me, but they may not be the blessings God chooses to entrust to them.

Here's an important takeaway for us: Heart Sisters appreciate one another's blessings, callings, and gifts and encourage each other to manage those blessings well.

Our last reading for today, which is one of my favorite stories in the Bible, involves the disciple Peter. Oh, Peter—how I identify with him! Jesus saw potential in Peter, but his zeal and tendency to speak before thinking often got him into trouble. In fact, Peter's denial that he knew Jesus—not once, not twice, but three times—serves as an important backstory to the verses we are going to read now.

Read John 21:15-19. In light of Peter's three-time denial of Jesus, what is significant about what happens in these verses?

Just as Peter denied Jesus three times, Jesus gave Peter three opportunities to affirm his love for Jesus. Clearly Jesus was giving Peter the chance to redeem himself. Don't you love that we serve a God of second chances? Jesus also was tasking Peter with his own "load"—to feed and care for His sheep—because He desired Peter to be a key leader of the early church (which, as we see in the Book of Acts, he helped to establish).

Now we come to my favorite part of the story.

Read John 21:20-23.

What does Peter notice?

What does he say to Jesus?

What is Jesus' reply?

Peter looked sideways at what John was doing rather than looking up to what God had planned for him. Can't we all identify with this?

After studying this passage for several years and reading endless commentaries, it has become one of my favorite moments in the Bible. When I find myself comparing who I am to others, I hear Jesus saying, "Natalie, what's it to you?"

"*You* follow *me*," He says.

Jesus speaks the same words to you, friend! If you will let go of the heavy load of comparison, you'll discover a freedom that can come only from accepting who God created you to be. This allows you to celebrate your own unique call from God as well as the path others have been called to follow—even if it isn't the same as your own! Breaking free from comparisons allows you to do just that: *break free*. And "wherever the Spirit of the Lord is, there is freedom" (2 Corinthians 3:17).

Turning to God

I often wonder why it's so easy to fall into the comparison trap—even when I know better. We live in a culture that seems to encourage us to be "every woman"—to have every hair in place with Pinterest-inspired meals on the table each night. We're supposed to pursue personal and professional development, keep up with the laundry, nurture relationships, and maintain a home that looks like the pages of a Pottery Barn catalog? Really? I'm exhausted just from writing those sentences!

Take a moment to rest in the Lord. Turn on your favorite worship song (for ideas, see the Spotify playlist referenced in the endnotes,[1] and ask Him to reveal what He has for *you*. Not your friends. Not your family. Not your coworkers. *You*.

> **What blessings has God entrusted to your care? What load or burdens are you carrying now? In the space below, journal or draw what you "hear," and be prepared to share it with at least one person in your group.**

DAY 2: BONE-ROTTING ENVY

Years ago a friend invited me over to see her new home. As soon as I walked through the door, I noticed it: an extreme absence of clutter.

I despise clutter. "Stuff" stresses me out. Yet at the time my husband and I had three very young children and a dog. Five people plus a big yellow

Labrador retriever equals a lot of stuff. When you have a lot of stuff, you eventually run out of room, and the stuff becomes clutter. Clutter makes me feel, well, cluttered.

I tried to be happy for my friend. Really, I did. However, I wanted what she had so badly that it was very hard for me to be joyful for her. It pains me to even type this because it's so ugly, but, alas, it is true.

I returned to our uber-cluttered home and let out our big, goofy dog who sheds everywhere, and suddenly I was overcome with even more "ugly": ingratitude and envy. I'm embarrassed to say that sometimes I have a very ungrateful heart for the many blessings God has bestowed upon me—blessings I don't deserve in the least. Yesterday, we talked about the sin of comparison, which separates us from God and hinders our relationships with others. And we can't talk about comparison without talking about envy, or jealousy.

Read Proverbs 14:30 in the margin. According to this verse, what is the result of envy?

A heart at peace gives life to the body,
but envy rots the bones.
(Proverbs 14:30 NIV)

I don't know about you, but to me a life-giving heart that is at peace sounds pretty good—much better than rotting bones. In fact, the Bible uses the Hebrew word *qin'ah* for this kind of envy. Synonyms of *qin'ah* are anger, jealousy, rivalry, and zeal.[2]

Envy is rooted in anger—anger that is rooted in ingratitude.

Read Ephesians 2:10 in the margin. How are we described in this verse?

For we are God's masterpiece. He has created us anew in Christ Jesus, so we can do the good things he planned for us long ago.
(Ephesians 2:10)

Take a moment to really think about this: you are God's masterpiece. Merriam-Webster's *New Collegiate Dictionary* defines a masterpiece as "the best book, painting, piece of music, movie, etc., by a particular person" and "something done with great skill."[3] The God of the entire universe considers you His greatest work because you were made with great skill. So, when we compare ourselves to others and become envious, we are putting down the work that God has done.

Remember, there is no condemnation in Christ Jesus (Romans 8:1). Comparison often leads to envy, and both are two very natural, human

When we compare ourselves to others and become envious, we are putting down the work that God has done.

emotions. It's just that when these two get together, they lead to destruction rather than construction. In other words, they tear down instead of build up.

Speaking of tearing down, let's return to the story of our friends Rachel and Leah. Goodness gracious, these ladies know all about comparison and envy, don't they?

Read Genesis 29:31-35. Why did God enable Leah to conceive and not Rachel?

On the line below, create a timeline of Leah's births. On one side, write the name of the birthed son. On the other side, write Leah's response to each birth.

Birthed Sons

Leah's Responses

Poor Leah. We can see that she hoped to win Jacob's love after her first three sons were born. Yet after she gave birth to her fourth son, she saw God's faithfulness and decided to praise Him instead of ask Him for something.

Being the most-loved wife may not have been God's plan for her, but bearing many sons—the highest honor for a woman at that time—was. In fact, Leah's six sons became six of the twelve tribes of Israel (more on how Leah's four sons became six in just a moment). Clearly, God had big plans for Leah all along—plans she couldn't see at the time.

Now, let's get into some serious biblical envy. Get ready, sisters.

Read Genesis 30:1-8.

According to verse 1, what was Rachel feeling, and what did she say to Jacob?

Fun Fact

Leah stopped and praised when Judah was born. The line of Judah is the line from which Jesus would come.

What was her solution to her inability to conceive?

What did she say in verse 8?

Scripture Challenge

Read Jeremiah 17:9 to find out what the Bible teaches about the human heart—the seat of our emotions.

There it is as clear as day: Rachel viewed Leah as competition—a game in which there were winners and losers. I'm guessing that Rachel had grown accustomed to receiving more attention than Leah. She was beautiful. Men noticed her. Beauty was, and still is, greatly valued, and it offered many opportunities to those blessed with loveliness. She probably didn't like feeling as though she was losing the "Who Can Bear Sons" game, so she took matters into her own hands and offered her handmaid Bilhah to Jacob. Then she claimed the sons her maid bore as her own. Whoever called the Bible boring?

Nonetheless, when Rachel began to claim her own sons, Leah became nervous because her fertility was her greatest asset in her marriage.

Read Genesis 30:9-13. What did Leah do, and what was the result?

Now read verses 14 and 15.

What did Rachel want?

How did Leah answer?

Would you say her tone was kind or unkind?

Fun Fact

In biblical times, many people held the superstitious belief that the mandrake root could help women who were unable to conceive to become pregnant. Barren women desiring children would either eat the roots in small amounts, wear them in an amulet around their necks, or place them beneath their beds in the hope they would conceive.[4]

I think it's clear these two women lived in a constant state of comparison and envy! Eventually, Leah made a deal with her sister: fresh mandrakes in exchange for a night with their husband. (That seems ridiculous to us, but check out the Fun Fact in the margin for more understanding.)

Leah conceived a son after Jacob slept with her, and Rachel soon became pregnant as well. Between Leah and Rachel and their maids Bilhah and Zilpah, Jacob fathered twelve sons, and these twelve sons eventually became the twelve tribes of Israel.

It makes me sad to think of Leah and Rachel. I know their circumstances were less than ideal; however, there wasn't much either could do to change those circumstances. Women during this time in history placed their security in their ability to have children; if they could not have children, they were thought to be cursed.

I wish Leah and Rachel could have lived together in sisterly love; however, their relationship exhibits the bone-rotting envy we read about in Proverbs 14:30. My guess is that the comparison that led to envy negatively impacted their lives every single day. What a sad way to live.

Before we end today, let's look at what James says about envy. James was Jesus' brother, and he never minced words. In a convicting and direct way, he shares wisdom and truth we all can benefit from reading.

Read James 3:13-17 and complete the chart below:

Heavenly wisdom is:	Earthly wisdom is:

Now read verse 18 and fill in the blanks below (your translation may be different).

Peacemakers who sow in peace reap a _____

of _____. *(NIV)*

Part of being a peacemaker is ridding our hearts of bone-rotting envy and comparison, and this is a process. However, with God's grace and mercy, we *can* break free from the chains of envy that so negatively impact our relationships!

Turning to God

How are you, sweet sister? I ask because when I first began to explore Scriptures on comparison and envy, I was appropriately convicted. I was also surprised to find that I did, indeed, have some envy in my heart. And I clearly had been prideful of my perceived lack of envy, which turned out to be grossly inaccurate!

Spend some time with God, and ask Him to search your heart for any envy that might be impacting your relationships—or you in general. Then ask Him to help you release it. You might have to repeat this process several times, and that's OK. Just keep releasing it, and begin to walk in the freedom that comes from breaking free of the chains of envy.

Now, write five things you are grateful for right now:

1.

2.

3.

4.

5.

Finally, name what makes you feel envious. Confess it aloud to God or write it on a notecard, or both. If you choose to write it, end your confession with these words: "What's it to you, (your name)?" If you write your confession on a notecard, place it somewhere you will see it often so that you will be reminded to keep your focus on the load and blessings that *you* carry.

DAY 3: LIFE-CHOKING INSECURITY

Remember when I mentioned on Day 1 how I once tried to fill the God-shaped hole in my heart with things of the world? That's because I failed to

> **Vulnerability gives others a glimpse into our hearts, communicating an authenticity that tears down the walls veiling who we really are.**

⁷ So to keep me from becoming proud, I was given a thorn in my flesh, a messenger from Satan to torment me and keep me from becoming proud. ⁸ Three different times I begged the Lord to take it away. ⁹ Each time he said, "My grace is all you need. My power works best in weakness." So now I am glad to boast about my weaknesses, so that the power of Christ can work through me. ¹⁰ That's why I take pleasure in my weaknesses, and in the insults, hardships, persecutions, and troubles that I suffer for Christ. For when I am weak, then I am strong.

(2 Corinthians 12:7-10)

understand not only *who* I was but also *whose* I was. I tried to base my identity on stuff from the world—stuff that can so easily be taken away. Instead, I needed to base my identity on the truth of who I am in God's eyes—a God who is the same yesterday, today, and tomorrow. When we choose to root our identity in who He says we are rather than who the world says we are, we can never be shaken. Those roots run deep and anchor us firmly into God's truth.

Comparison and envy conspire together to erode our identity, and before we know it, we've become a shell of uncertainty—insecure and lacking in confidence.

How do we get to this point? I believe it happens when we adopt the thinking of our self-absorbed culture. Ever since Eve and Adam ate the apple, we've all been predisposed to selfishness (though it's true that some of us can become more self-absorbed than others). Now, take this natural tendency and place it in our "Selfie" culture, and you have an "It's all about me" mind-set. This attitude has become so common that I've actually seen T-shirts with those words emblazoned across the chest!

However, we don't have to wear the T-shirt to be infected by the attitude—whether consciously or subconsciously. It can be so subtle. We see something enticing that belongs to someone else—be it a new car, a group of friends, or a big, beautiful home (clutter-free, of course)—and we find ourselves comparing and becoming envious. And if we compare too much, it's likely we will begin to be envious. Too much comparison, and envy can attack the roots of even the most firmly planted believer, eroding her security.

In a culture that tells us "It's all about me" while encouraging more, more, and more, we face a steep challenge. But it's not an impossible challenge, sisters. Sharing our own insecurities brings them out of the darkness into the light, and there God can do His best healing work. Vulnerability gives others a glimpse into our hearts, communicating an authenticity that tears down the walls veiling who we really are.

We all have "stuff" that can create our own insecurities. These insecurities might lead us to hesitate before we allow ourselves to be vulnerable—both external and internal challenges. Let's look at what the Apostle Paul said about a personal challenge of his own and how he handled it.

Read 2 Corinthians 12:7-10 in the margin. Why was Paul given a "thorn"?

Why would God not want Paul to become conceited?

How can our own challenges—whether external or internal—keep us from becoming conceited or proud? Give an example from your own life, if possible.

If we don't have a need for God, we won't have a lead from God.

Paul's thorn exemplifies a broader basic truth. If we don't have a need for God, we won't have a lead from God. In other words, unless we have something that drives us to God, we risk losing our motivation for allowing Him to lead us through life.

When visiting Ghana several years ago, I was in awe of the people, who have so little yet so much. While they aren't always sure when they will next eat and they lack the conveniences we often take for granted, I found them to be a very faithful and joyful people. Their need for God keeps them close to God. Similarly, only when we recognize our great need for God do we rely completely on His provisions for the challenges we face, acknowledging that we can't make it alone. Those challenges or "thorns" are the very things God uses to show the world what He can do.

Look again at 2 Corinthians 12:9-10 in the margin. What did God tell Paul, and how did Paul respond?

Why do you think people tend to relate to our struggles and failures more than they do our successes?

Think of a challenging time when perhaps you felt that you failed. What did you learn about God during that time?

Our thorns can drive us to God, or they can overtake us and lead to full-blown insecurity.

God knows we will fall short. In fact, the Greek word for sin, *hamartano´*, actually means "to miss the mark."[5] God knows that we often miss the mark and need Him—every single day. Thankfully, the grace granted to us through His Son, Jesus, covers those missed marks. As Paul said, God's grace is sufficient, and when we are weak, He is strong indeed!

Like Paul, we have our own external or internal challenges—thorns. Our thorns can drive us to God, or they can overtake us and lead to full-blown insecurity. Sometimes we allow our thorns to choke the life out of the roots we have established in God's truth. Or maybe we've never grown roots in God's truth but have anchored our roots in things of this world. Either way, insecurity occurs when we water the thorns more than the roots.

There's an old Native American story about a Cherokee grandfather who told his grandson of a battle between two wolves within each of us. He explained that one of the wolves is evil. It is envious, jealous, and proud. The other wolf is good. It is joyful, peaceful, and kind. After the grandson thought about this for a while, he asked his grandfather, "Which wolf wins?" The grandfather responded, "The one you feed."

If we feed the thorns instead of the roots, we'll reap insecurity every time. But if we feed the roots—the truths of God's Word—we'll reap peace, kindness, and joy.

What is a "thorn" that is reaping insecurity in your life?

Because the remedy to life-choking insecurity is God's truth, we are going to close today by resting in the truths of Psalm 139. This psalm, which is one of my favorites, tells us so much about who we are in God's eyes.

So that we may really think about what we're reading, I want to introduce you to one of my favorite methods of reading and praying Scripture: *Lectio Divina*.

Lectio Divina is a Latin phrase meaning "divine reading."[6] It's a slow and thoughtful reading of Scripture through which one enters a conversation with God. This ancient practice that dates back to early monastic communities has been passed on generation to generation and is reemerging today as a wonderful way to hear and experience the Word of God.

Read through the following steps, and then conclude your study today by trying *Lectio Divina* with Psalm 139.

Steps to *Lectio Divina*

Ask the Holy Spirit to protect you, lead you, and help you to let go of your own agenda so that you can listen to what He wants you to hear. Slowly read the text through four times. With each reading, ask a different question.

1. Read (*Lectio*)—Read the passage. What word or phrase stands out to me?

2. Reflect (*Meditatio*)—Read again. What in the text touches my life or relates to it in some way?

3. Respond (*Oratio*)—Read again. What is God inviting me to do or be? How is He asking me to respond?

4. Rest (*Contemplatio*)—Read again, and rest in God's loving presence.

Lectio Divina Exercise

Pray for God's guidance, and then read Psalm 139 four times, each time pausing to listen and record your responses:

1. Read (*Lectio*) – What word or phrase stands out to me?

2. Reflect (*Meditatio*)—What in the text touches my life or relates to it in some way?

3. Respond (*Oratio*)—What is God inviting me to do or be? How is He asking me to respond?

4. Rest (*Contemplatio*)—Read again and rest in God's loving presence.

Turning to God

Why is it so difficult sometimes for us to believe how much God loves us? Often when I think of how much He has forgiven me and how treasured I am in His eyes, I become overwhelmed by His mercy. You've already spent some time with God today through *Lectio Divina*, but now take a moment and ask God to help you to remember who you are and whose you are (fearfully and wonderfully made, cherished, daughter of the Most High King, and so forth). Record what you hear below.

DAY 4: SNEAKY PRIDE

Once upon a time, when someone admitted to me she was being prideful, I remember thinking, "I'm so glad I don't struggle with pride. I don't brag or boast, and I don't think I'm the greatest thing since sliced bread. Clearly, I don't have a problem with pride."

Do you see the irony of this thought? I was prideful about my lack of pride. I didn't quite understand that pride comes in many forms, which makes it a very sneaky sin. (By the way, if it's sneaky, it's not from God. Deception never, ever comes from Him.) In fact, once you can identify the many forms of pride, it's amazing how often you'll see it elsewhere. Pride is frequently the source of conflict, and it's rooted in fear—which we'll talk more about tomorrow.

The Bible is chock-full of instances in which pride gets in the way, and God has much to say to us about this sneaky little sin. Let's read what God has to say about pride. We're going to do some jumping around today, but I promise it will be worth it!

Look up each verse, and write what it says pride will do.

Verse:	What pride will do:
Deuteronomy 8:14	
2 Chronicles 26:16	
Proverbs 11:2	
Proverbs 13:10	
Proverbs 16:18	
Proverbs 29:23	
Obadiah 1:13	

Pretty unpleasant, eh? Now, let's look at what the Bible says about pride's antidote: humility.

Look up each verse, and write what you learn about humility:

Verse:	What it teaches about humility:
2 Chronicles 7:14	
Psalm 149:4	
Proverbs 11:2	
Proverbs 18:12	
Proverbs 22:4	
Proverbs 29:23	
James 4:10	

Pride is the "great thief" because it steals relationships, personal growth, and joy.

Pretty clear, right? More of Him, less of me. The Apostle John says it this way: "He must become greater and greater, and I must become less and less" (John 3:30).

Knowing how sneaky it is, how do we know if we're struggling with pride? After all, if you're like me, you might be too prideful to see your own pride!

Pride is the stubborn mule that makes us believe the other person should apologize to us because we've done nothing wrong. It's also responsible for tricking us into believing that once someone has wounded us, that someone doesn't deserve the benefits of reconciliation—even if the offender is humble and seeks forgiveness.

Pride is the "great thief" because it steals relationships, personal growth, and joy—just to name a few. It "prides" itself on its sneaky style and infiltrates our very beings through the ways of the world and the lies we are led to believe.

Pride also is essentially the fear of others seeing that we don't actually have it all together or figured out. It's an air we put on to distract others from knowing us authentically, and it blocks our ability to be vulnerable. Vulnerability is a product of humility, and humility is the foundation of all healthy relationships. Therefore, we can conclude that if vulnerability results from humility and humility is the foundation of all relationships, then the ability to be vulnerable is essential to achieving meaningful relationships. Pride will force you to hide your true self and separate you from those you love.

When we refuse to accept help, especially when we really need it, we are the victims of pride. When we overschedule ourselves because we've said yes too many times, often it is because we think we are the only ones who can do the tasks well—and yes, this is pride, too.

When we tirelessly minister to someone at the expense of our families and grow frustrated when the person doesn't act the way we think he or she should, we are the victims of pride. We can't be Jesus to anyone. Only Jesus can be Jesus! The only role we are to play is that of an obedient servant, who fulfills what God has called us to do; then we are to sit back and allow the Holy Spirit to do what only He can do.

The best way to combat pride is to humble ourselves—first to God, then to others. Like Paul, if we choose to reveal our weaknesses, we show both our humanity and the power of God. It's necessary to share about our thorns, admitting that we don't know everything or have it all together or live in a state of perfection. We must give ourselves permission to be vulnerable, especially to God. He is fully aware of our struggles, disappointments, and hurts, so revealing these things to Him won't be telling Him anything He doesn't already know.

In the space below, write three insights about pride and humility from the Scriptures we've read today that have resonated with you, and put a star next to the one that speaks to your heart the most:

1.

2.

3.

Why do you think this insight speaks to you?

Fun Fact

Uzziah's name means "My strength is Yah" (Yhovah).[7]

Let's wrap up our study today by reading about a king whose own struggle with pride led to a premature end of his reign.

Read 2 Chronicles 26:1-15. How would you describe King Uzziah after reading these verses?

Uzziah was an early eighth-century B.C. king from the tribe of Judah. (Yes, that's the tribe of Leah's son, Judah. Our worlds are coming together this week, aren't they?) During his reign, the kingdom of Judah experienced its greatest growth and prosperity since the reign of Solomon. He was a very beloved king and obviously cared about his kingdom greatly.

Unfortunately, his story takes a downward turn in verse 16.

Read 2 Chronicles 26:16-23 and answer the following questions.

What led to Uzziah's downfall? (v. 16)

How did he sin against God? (v. 16)

How did the priests react? (v. 18)

How did Uzziah react? (v. 19)

What happened as Uzziah was having this reaction? (v. 19)

Uzziah's power led him to believe that he was above the law. We see this often in our culture these days, don't we? Celebrities, politicians, and ordinary people make not-so-great-choices because they don't think they'll be punished—and sometimes they aren't. Yet our God is a holy God who disciplines those he loves (Hebrews 12:6), and so He allows us to experience the consequences of our sins (and there are always consequences with sin). In Uzziah's case, the consequence of his pride was physical illness—specifically, with leprosy—which led to his removal as king.

Pride comes before a fall indeed.

"Where is the love and grace?" you may wonder. We aren't told how long Uzziah acted proudly, how many sins his pride led him to commit against God, or how many times he hardened his heart and refused to listen to correction. As we read in verse 19, it wasn't until he became furious and raged at the priests that he was struck with leprosy. Imagine how differently his story might have ended if, after hearing their words of conviction, he had humbled himself and repented.

19 Now repent of your sins and turn to God, so that your sins may be wiped away. 20 Then times of refreshment will come from the presence of the Lord.

(Acts 3:19-20a)

Read Acts 3:19 in the margin. Why are we to repent of our sins, and what happens when we do?

But if we confess our sins to him, he is faithful and just to forgive us our sins and to cleanse us from all wickedness.

(1 John 1:9)

Now read 1 John 1:9 in the margin. What does this verse promise God will do when we confess our sins to Him?

Our God longs to restore us to right relationship with Him. If we humble ourselves, seek His forgiveness, and repent, God always gives us the grace and mercy we do not deserve.

Pride is a hard topic to discuss, isn't it? Each of us struggles with pride to some extent, because we all struggle with the sins of the flesh. You might say that we're disabled by the flesh. Though we might be flesh-disabled, we also are God-enabled. Let us turn to God and ask Him to help us with our pride, because our relationships—with God and with others—are just too valuable to let them succumb to this sneaky sin.

Turning to God

Sit with God for a few moments and ask Him to help you heal the broken places within that lead to pride. If you find yourself struggling with pride today, I challenge you to ask yourself what you're trying to hide and why. Then ask God to help you humble yourself, because pride's antidote is humility. End your time by giving thanks for God's great grace and mercy. If you like, write a prayer or your thoughts in the margin.

DAY 5: PARALYZING FEAR

You've made it to Day 5, friend! I know we've talked about some pretty hard stuff this week, but working through these sins that hinder our relationship with God will only bring us closer to our Creator, which is what we want. It's what He wants, too! And as I've said previously, getting right with God is the first step in cultivating authentic relationships, because it's hard to keep our relationships in sync when our relationship with God is out of sync.

So far we've discussed comparison, envy, insecurity, and pride. At the root of each of these sins is one very powerful culprit: fear. And though we don't tend to think of fear as a sin, it is. Have you ever noticed how often in the Bible we're commanded not to fear? (We're also commanded in the Bible to fear God, but in that context the word refers to a healthy reverence for God, not dread or terror.)

Like pride, fear is so sneaky that we often don't realize we're afraid until we are neck-deep in a spiral of lies that we have believed. You see, fear is never, ever from God.

> **Fear is a powerful enemy of faith, because it paralyzes us into inaction, reducing our effectiveness for the Kingdom.**

Read 2 Timothy 1:7. I prefer the New Living Translation or King James Version of this verse because they use the word *fear*. Write the verse below:

Fear is a powerful enemy of faith, because it paralyzes us into inaction, reducing our effectiveness for the Kingdom. Often it seems that the more we do for the kingdom of God, the more we find ourselves confronted with fear.

There was once a time when I was tempted to throw up my hands and proclaim I wasn't going to do anything for God and just fly under the radar because things had become so difficult. However, I was led to a Scripture that reminded me of the power of the God I serve.

Read 1 John 4:16-19.

How does this passage describe God? (v. 16)

What does it tell us about those who live in love? (vv. 16-17)

What does perfect love do? (v. 18)

If God is love and perfect love expels all fear, then we can logically conclude that God expels all fear! When we experience God's love, we have no reason to fear. And the deeper our relationship with the Lord, the more we are filled with His perfect love, which then spills out onto others. This love has no room for fear.

Unfortunately, we live in a fear-based culture. Just watch or read the news, and it's easy to be gripped by fear as we hear about frightening events and read devastating headlines. Unspeakable tragedies occur every day, and we must remain sensitive and compassionate, praying and doing what we can as God calls us to action. However, we must be careful not to succumb to fearmongering. We need to be wise about who we allow to control our fear-o-meter. Fear-based news gets better ratings than peaceful news.

After having three babies within four years, my husband and I went on a much-needed vacation to Mexico. We were excited and also a little nervous about leaving our children for the first time, but our desire to sit on the beach was much more powerful than that slight worry.

Two days after our arrival in Mexico, we received a frantic e-mail message from my mother: "Do you think you should come home? The swine flu outbreak there is horrible, and I'm so concerned!"

We had finally gone on an adult-only vacation, and our destination was the place where the swine flu epidemic began—while we were there. Awesome.

We investigated my mother's concerns, but no one seemed very worried. Sure, we had to use hand sanitizer when we arrived at the airport for our return flight, and everyone was required to take their temperature before boarding their plane; but other than that, it was business as usual.

When we returned home, I understood why my mother was concerned. The news made it sound as if people were dying all over Mexico every hour, every day!

According to the Anxiety and Depression Association of America, anxiety disorders are the most common mental illness in the United States. In fact, over 40 million people suffer from some form of anxiety; that's 18 percent of the population.[8] Any idea what can be found at the root of anxiety? That's right: fear.

So, what can we do when we're faced with fear? Though it's not easy, with God's help we can defeat fear by making two proactive choices.

1. Choose to not allow fear to control your thoughts. I know this may sound simplistic; however, we do have control over our thoughts. Will we focus our minds on things that bring peace or things that bring anxiety?

Read 2 Corinthians 10:5 in the margin. What does this verse instruct us to do?

Now read Philippians 4:8. On what things are we to fix our thoughts?

We demolish arguments and every pretension that sets itself up against the knowledge of God, and we take captive every thought to make it obedient to Christ.

(2 Corinthians 10:5 NIV)

And now, dear brothers and sisters, one final thing. Fix your thoughts on what is true, and honorable, and right, and pure, and lovely, and admirable. Think about things that are excellent and worthy of praise.

(Philippians 4:8)

When fear knocks on your door, remind yourself of what is true rather than thinking about what isn't. Fear subsides when we tune out the loud lies that beckon us and listen to the gentle, loving voice of God. Focusing our thoughts on God's truth and His perfect, unfailing love drives out fear.

2. Choose to guard your heart.

Read Proverbs 4:23. What does this verse tell us to do and why?

If watching the news makes your blood pressure rise, then stop watching the news. I stopped watching it years ago, and trust me, I still find out about current events. If spending time with people who also struggle with fear sets you off, then implement a boundary and limit your time with those individuals. If watching certain movies or television shows or reading particular books increases your fear response—you guessed it—stay away. Above all else, guard your heart!

One of the best ways to guard your heart is to fortify it with God's truth about fear by reading, studying, and memorizing Scripture—and then praying that the Holy Spirit will guide and protect you.

Take a moment to look up the verses below. Write a short summary of each, or you may prefer to write out the verse.

Exodus 14:14

Deuteronomy 31:6

Joshua 1:9

Psalm 56:3

Proverbs 12:25

Isaiah 41:10

1 Peter 5:7

Choose the two verses that speak to you the most, and draw a star beside them.

Though technically these verses are about fear, I hope you also discovered another theme: hope. In His perfect love, God is the great restorer of hope. He makes all things new. He can do so much with so little. Nothing is ever beyond His capabilities! I'm sure you know this truth, sweet friend, but sometimes we just need to hear it again. I know I do!

Now, what if you try these two suggestions and still don't feel better? Sometimes repetition and persistence will bring a breakthrough. But if you make these two choices for some time and are still struggling with fear, you may be dealing with anxiety or depression, which are physiological conditions related to brain chemistry. No one should ever be ashamed of suffering from either of these conditions. We don't tell someone who wears glasses she just needs to have more faith so she can see better, do we? Of course not! If you think anxiety or depression is a struggle for you, please speak to a medical professional or counselor so that you can get the help you need to break free from fear.

This week we've explored five common sins that inhibit our relationship with God—and consequently affect our relationships with others. Along the way we've considered strategies that can help us to overcome these obstacles to authentic relationship. To tie it all together, I'd like to highlight five important habits that can help us to get right with God—and others.

1. Pray often. You can't have a relationship with someone you don't talk to very often, right? Talk to God. Thank Him. Cry out to Him. He already knows what's going on in your heart; He just wants you to say it to Him. God's got big shoulders. He can handle anything you throw at Him!

2. Spend time with God. You can't have a very authentic relationship with someone you don't spend much time with. Spending time with God might look different for you than it would for me. We may not have our "quiet time" at the same time. We may not read the same materials. What matters most is that you spend time with God each day.

3. Worship. Worshiping God doesn't have to be limited to Sundays! Stream worship music through your home or put on some headphones on the job if you can. It's amazing how much more positive and refreshed I feel after listening to worship music.

4. Go to church. Even if you've been hurt by the church, we're still called to be in community with other believers as part of a church body. After my husband and I experienced this ourselves, we were devastated. However, we learned a very valuable lesson: church is just one piece of the faith puzzle, and it's led by sinners like you and me. However, it also should be noted that church is a very valuable piece of the faith puzzle. The best place to find a community of other believers is church—broken people and all.

5. Forgive those who have hurt you. This is a big one—so big that this topic has its own week in our study. We'll talk more about forgiveness later, but let me just whet your appetite a bit: we don't forgive to benefit the one who hurt us; we forgive for our own benefit. Unforgiveness leads to anger, resentment, and bitterness—even toward God. Release it, forgive, and move on.

Well, friend, you made it through a very important week of study that will be foundational to all that is to come. It's critical to identify the toxins that can negatively impact our relationships so that we can overcome them. Congratulations! Identifying the "junk" is half the battle. You did it! Nothing excites me more than the imaginary clamor of chains falling to the ground after letting go of negative weight that holds us back!

Turning to God

Take a moment and thank God for His truly amazing grace and love. God doesn't expect us to change or heal overnight; in fact, God heals us one layer at a time. I'm so thankful He doesn't just rip off the bandage, aren't you? *Thank You, God, for the unending grace that You so freely give because You are love! Amen.*

GETTING RIGHT WITH GOD

If my own people will humbly pray and turn back to me and stop sinning, then I will answer them from heaven. I will forgive them and make their land fertile once again.

(2 Chronicles 7:14 CEV)

If we can't humble ourselves before _____, it's going to be difficult to humble

ourselves before _____ _____.

If we confess our sins, he is faithful and just and will forgive us our sins and purify us from all unrighteousness.

(1 John 1:9 NIV)

Our relationship with God is the _____ that sets the

_____ of our relationship with others.

Comparison happens when we look _____ at other people instead

of _____ _____ to God.

If anyone thinks they are something when they are not, they deceive themselves. Each one should test their own actions. Then they can take pride in themselves alone, without comparing themselves to someone else, for each one should carry their own load.

(Galatians 6:3-5 NIV)

Comparison almost always leads to _____.

VIDEO VIEWER GUIDE: WEEK 2

God doesn't intend for us to further His kingdom _____. He intends for us

all, as believers, to work together as _____ _____.

Many Parts, One Body

[12] Just as a body, though one, has many parts, but all its many parts form one body, so it is with Christ. [13] For we were all baptized by[a] one Spirit so as to form one body—whether Jews or Gentiles, slave or free—and we were all given the one Spirit to drink. [14] Even so the body is not made up of one part but of many.

[15] Now if the foot should say, "Because I am not a hand, I do not belong to the body," it would not for that reason stop being part of the body. [16] And if the ear should say, "Because I am not an eye, I do not belong to the body," it would not for that reason stop being part of the body. [17] If the whole body were an eye, where would the sense of hearing be? If the whole body were an ear, where would the sense of smell be? [18] But in fact God has placed the parts in the body, every one of them, just as he wanted them to be. [19] If they were all one part, where would the body be? [20] As it is, there are many parts, but one body.

(1 Corinthians 12:12-20 NIV)

_____ often leads to _____.

Comparison + Pride + Envy = Insecurity

All the players of this equation work together to eventually create _____.

When our souls are insecure because of comparison, envy, and/or pride,

we find ourselves living in _____ of things that may never even

_____.

Week 3

CLASH OF THE TITANS

HONORING GOD THROUGH
RELATIONAL CONFLICT

Memory Verse

If it is possible, as far as it depends on you, live at peace with everyone.
(Romans 12:18 NIV)

Just Between Us

Have you seen the movie *Clash of the Titans*? The original movie was released in 1981 and was remade in 2010. This action-adventure movie is the fictional story of the notorious conflict between the Greek gods Perseus, Zeus, and Hades—who all happened to be siblings. Though Greek mythology is based in narratives that are purely fictional, the idea of being in conflict is neither fictional nor foreign to us. Anyone who has ever been in an authentic relationship with another person has experienced relational conflict at some point. Whenever beautifully yet uniquely created people come together in relationship, there is bound to be some conflict.

Does the idea of conflict make you want to run far, far away? If so, you're not alone, sister. I don't like conflict, either. Not many people do. However, sometimes we allow our fear of conflict to determine the way we handle it. We're often tempted to sweep it under the rug, telling ourselves we're overreacting. Though sometimes we may, in fact, be overreacting (we'll talk about that this week), we sometimes use that as an excuse in order to avoid having a hard conversation. Trust me; I know all about it! Been there, done that. Have several of the T-shirts.

The problem is that conflict can fester when we sweep it under the rug. If ignored, conflict can lead to a bitter root and eventually destroy the friendship. I experienced this myself several years ago when a friend and I had a falling out about a ministry in which we were both serving. She saw things one way; I saw them another. After we were able to take a step back from the situation, we were able to have a good heart-to-heart—and we are stronger friends now because of it.

I think many of our hurts can be healed over a cup of coffee if we take the time to really listen to each other—as in focusing on what our friend is saying rather than outlining our defense as she's speaking. I'm not so "pie in the sky" to think that all conflicts can be resolved over a heartfelt conversation, but I believe that many of them can.

Part of the reason we're so scared of conflict is that we don't know how to deal with conflict. This week we'll learn how to navigate conflict in a way that honors God and preserves the relationship. When we handle conflict in this way, it's possible to become even closer Heart Sisters because of the conflict!

DAY 1: CAN WE JUST ALL GET ALONG?

Years ago, a friend from my youth and I had a falling out. We had been friends for many years, so it was incredibly painful when we parted ways. We were young, immature, and selfish when our disagreement ripped our friendship apart. In full disclosure, I struggled over this lost relationship for several years. What could I have done differently? What should I do now? What was my part in this conflict?

Ten years later, I found myself married with an eighteen-month-old daughter. As my husband gave her a bath, our phone rang. It was the friend from my youth.

"Natalie, I wanted to call you because you've been on my mind so much. I'm moving back to the area, and I've always felt like I should apologize to you. I'm so sorry for what happened, and I just wanted to ask you for your forgiveness," she said.

I was dumbfounded. Never in a million years did I expect to receive that call.

I proceeded to apologize for my own role in our disagreement, and we made plans to meet for dinner a few days later.

We laughed so much during that dinner—after all, we had a lot of catching up to do! It brought me such joy and peace to know that the relationship I once treasured was finally reconciled.

I know not all stories of hurt end up like this one, friend. Disagreements don't always conclude with a pretty, red bow on top, do they? Yet as long as we are all created differently, as long as we all have free will, as long as we live in a world infected with sin, we will have conflict.

Does just thinking about conflict make you break out into a cold sweat? Do you want to run to the nearest corner, suck your thumb, and rock back and forth until it all goes away? Would you rather have a root canal than a difficult conversation?

If you answered yes to these questions, I understand completely. Few of us enjoy conflict, right?

Read John 16:33 in the margin.

What did Jesus say we would have in this world?

"I have told you all this so that you may have peace in me. Here on earth you will have many trials and sorrows. But take heart, because I have overcome the world."

(John 16:33)

What reassurance did he offer us?

According to this verse, who offers us peace?

How does Jesus offer us peace? We know that He's the answer to all of our troubles, but sometimes we just don't see how He's going to help with that difficult person in our lives or assist us with a hard conversation.

What do you think of when you think of peace? Draw or write your description below.

Here's the thing: even though Jesus can't be with us physically—we can't have him over for dinner or meet Him for coffee when we're having a bad day—He *truly does* help us with our tough relationships and hard conversations. How? After He went to be with the Father, He sent His Spirit to live within us and help us—when we're troubled and when we're not.

I've recently become a *Star Wars* fan as I've watched the movies through the eyes of my children. Luke and several other Jedi knights are always encouraged to "use the force"—an unseen power that can defend and protect in harrowing situations. Though it's a very limited and flawed analogy, you could say that in a sense the Holy Spirit is our "force"—yet He is so, so much more!

We need the force of Jesus in our relationships because it is the Spirit living in us that guides and empowers us to do what is right in the eyes of the Lord.

Read John 14:26. How does this verse describe what the Holy Spirit does for us?

But when the Father sends the Advocate as my representative— that is, the Holy Spirit— he will teach you everything and will remind you of everything I have told you.

(John 14:26)

The Holy Spirit is literally God, who dwells in us. He is our teacher and our guide, who helps us to do what will glorify Him. And nothing glorifies God more beautifully than peace among His people.

As it turns out, Jesus is there for us during relational conflict, because if we've chosen to follow Him, the Spirit of God lives within us. He's a part of us. Thank you, Lord. Now that's what I call comfort!

If Jesus is our peace, then let's look at what He says about obtaining peace.

In the chart below, summarize or write each verse.

Psalm 34:14	
Proverbs 16:7	
Isaiah 26:3	
John 14:27	
Philippians 4:6-7	

Based on this chart, what are three things we can learn about peace?

1.

2.

3.

Put a star beside the one that speaks to you most. Why do you think this resonates with you?

According to Psalm 34:14 in the margin, what are we supposed to do with peace?

Turn away from evil and do good.
Search for peace, and work to maintain it.
(Psalm 34:14)

What do you think this means?

Heart Sisters are peacemakers, not peace-takers. However, sometimes we can confuse the two, so it is important to understand the true definition of peace. According to Ken Sande, author of *The Peacemaker: A Biblical Guide to Resolving Personal Conflict* and president of Peacemaker Ministries, "When Christians become peacemakers, they can turn conflict into an opportunity to strengthen relationships and make their lives a testimony to the love and power of Jesus Christ."[1] Peacemakers don't just sweep it under the rug and hope it goes away. Peacemakers understand the long-term risks of that way of thinking and, instead, choose to pursue peace so that the relationship can be healthy and God-honoring.

Those who pursue peace

- seek to talk through a conflict with humility.
- aren't afraid to say "I was hurt."
- are truthful when asked if they were hurt.
- don't let things go because of fear of conflict.
- recognize the importance of clearing up misunderstandings, because most offenses aren't intentional.

Choosing not to discuss unintentional hurt is an intentional way to end a friendship.

Does that last one hit a nerve with you? It certainly did with me! In my own experience, I've found that most people I've approached about what I perceived to be an offense did not even realize their actions or words had been hurtful to me. The reverse is true as well. When I've been approached because I've hurt someone, either by my words or actions, I oftentimes have not been aware of the offense.

A few years ago, a friend of mine made a comment about me that really stung, but I was concerned that maybe I was making a mountain out of molehill. Yet every time I was with her, I was reminded of what she had said.

Eventually I realized I needed to tell her that I had been hurt by her words. She felt horrible, having no idea that she had hurt me, because her words had been intended to mean something different from what I had heard.

Can you imagine if I had continued to harbor that hurt and rejection? No doubt I would have begun to distance myself from my friend, and she not only would be confused but also hurt. If I had not mustered the courage to speak to her (which came only from God, let me assure you!), I'm not sure our friendship would still be alive and well today. Choosing not to discuss unintentional hurt is an intentional way to end a friendship.

Lest we think relational conflict is a modern-day affliction, let's take a look at a conflict that happened to Paul and Barnabas in the Book of Acts.

Read Acts 13:13 in the margin. Who left Paul and his ministry companions?

Paul and his companions then left Paphos by ship for Pamphylia, landing at the port town of Perga. There John Mark left them and returned to Jerusalem.

(Acts 13:13)

Paul, Barnabas, and John Mark were about to embark upon a journey to Perga in Pamphylia, some four hundred miles from Jerusalem. There were fewer Jewish believers in Perga than in Cypress, where they had previously shared the gospel. Fewer Jewish believers often meant more pagans, and more pagans often meant hearts that were closed to the teachings of Jesus. In other words, it was going to be a rough crowd!

Paul and Barnabas continued their ministry through seven different cities, facing persecution and disbelief from the pagan crowd. However, both men became known as an encouraging and wise duo who blessed many through the sharing of the gospel.

Now read Acts 15:36-41. Why did Paul and Barnabas disagree? How did they solve this disagreement?

Fun Fact

At first glance a new believer might think that Timothy wrote 1 and 2 Timothy, but it was actually Paul who authored these books as letters to Timothy.

Have you ever had to part ways with a family member or friend? How did that experience affect you?

It's horribly painful to part ways with someone we love—even if it's the healthiest choice. Often conflict brings out the worst in us because we so easily become preoccupied with being right, justifying our position, or feeling guilty.

Read 2 Timothy 4:11. What did Paul say about John Mark in his letter to Timothy?

Somewhere during the course of Paul's continued ministry, he arrived at a place of peace with John Mark and was able to give him a second chance.

Relational conflict does not have to last forever. As we'll learn next week, reconciliation occurs on God's timetable; we need only to be still, pay attention to the nudges from the Holy Spirit, and pursue peace. *Even when it's hard.*

Turning to God

Take a moment to reflect upon a conflict that led to a parting of ways with another person. If you have never experienced this personally, think of a relationship between people you know who have parted ways. What sin led to this conflict? Pray for the other person (or those involved), and humbly ask God to bring healing. God knows our hearts inside and out. Ask Him to search your heart and show you where you were wrong.

God also knows the hearts of our "enemies," which is why we need to pray for them too. Pray for all parties involved, forgiving all offenses and releasing the entire situation to God. If you are not involved directly, pray for those who are. We all benefit when those we know are at peace with one another.

DAY 2: RELATIONAL CONFLICT IN THE BIBLE

A few days ago, a friend of mine and I were lamenting over relational conflict, saying that we just can't wait for Jesus to return so we don't have to experience it anymore. "Do you think we've always had such conflict, or do you think this is a result of living in a technology-saturated culture where we interact with others less?" my friend asked.

After my friend posed this question, she quickly answered it herself: conflict is nothing new. In fact, conflict first entered the world the moment Eve took a bite out of the forbidden fruit. The serpent planted a seed of doubt, and Eve fell for it. Without meaning to, she created a relational conflict between herself and God. Just to be clear, Adam also ate the fruit, so he was involved in the conflict too. He even blamed Eve, no doubt creating a conflict between the two of them!

Yesterday we talked about Paul and Barnabas's dispute over John Mark. Today we're going to discuss a few other instances of relational conflict in the Bible.

Read Matthew 21:1-11. In one or two sentences, describe what was happening:

Continue reading verses 12 and 13.

Where was Jesus?

Why was He angry?

Whose tables did Jesus specifically turn over?

Jesus entered Jerusalem as the King for the first time. As was typical in those days, the king's processional would travel through the city and end at the Temple, where there would be a sacrifice or a banquet in his honor. Instead, Jesus found merchants buying and selling in the Temple courts.

Now read Leviticus 5:7. What were the poor to bring as a sacrifice if they couldn't afford a lamb?

Jesus overturned the tables of the moneychangers and those selling doves because they were selling to the poor. Some scholars believe Jesus' righteous anger may have been prompted by injustices against the poor.

Read Matthew 21:14-17.

Who became indignant with Jesus? Why do you think this was so?

Have you ever struggled with anger or known someone who has? Anger in general is a sin. However, righteous anger, the kind Jesus expressed in the Temple, is not. It's important to note this distinction because at some point we will experience anger in our relationships—either as the one who is angry or the one to whom another's anger is directed. And the distinction is a good sieve to use when sifting or monitoring anger—our own and that of others.

If our anger is generated by outright sin, then it is righteous anger, which demands an appropriate, God-honoring response. However, we must always seek God's direction before giving expression to righteous anger, asking for specific guidance in when and how to respond. (Righteous anger never gives us liberty to sin.) As we see in Matthew 21:14-17, even an appropriate demonstration of righteous anger can reap relational conflict if those involved do not respond with humble and repentant hearts. Although Jesus was without sin when he turned over the tables, the priests and teachers chose to respond with indignation rather than humility. Their example shows us that when we are guilty of sin and find ourselves on the receiving end of righteous anger, we need to humble ourselves and seek God's face rather than becoming defensive or lashing out.

If, on the other hand, our anger is not generated by sin but is the result of our own selfishness—such as not getting our way or wanting something we can't have because we aren't in control—then it is unrighteous anger, and we must acknowledge it and let it go. And when the unrighteous anger of someone else is being directed toward us, we do not have to participate in it. We can choose, instead, to respond with love and grace.

Think about the last time you were angry. Was it righteous or unrighteous anger? Describe it below:

If it was unrighteous anger, take a moment to confess it to God and ask Him for forgiveness.

What can we learn from unrighteous anger? Record a few thoughts below:

Another one of my favorite stories of conflict in the Bible involves Abram's wife, Sarai, and her maidservant, Hagar.

Read Genesis 16:1-2.

What was Sarai's desire and how did she decide to fulfill it?

How did Abram respond?

This all sounds a little crazy by today's standards, doesn't it? Yet at that time a barren woman offering her husband a mistress to produce a child was a common cultural practice. Thankfully this is no longer the case in most cultures today, because nothing good comes from polygamy or adultery, sisters—as we're about to see.

Continue reading verses 3-6.

What happened when Hagar became pregnant?

How did Hagar and Sarai each feel and act?

Interesting turn of events, isn't it? Whoever called the Bible dull! Sarai is the one who came up with this not-so-great plan, taking matters into her own hands. However, she didn't consider the resentment that would surface within Hagar. Goodness gracious! And Abram? He pretty much walked away from it all. I can just picture him shaking his head and muttering under his breath after that conversation.

Read Genesis 16:7-15.

Who found Hagar, and what did he tell her to do?

What did he promise her, and what did he tell her about the child she would birth?

How did Hagar respond? What did she say to God?

Because Sarai decided to take control instead of trusting God to bless her and Abram with a biological child, a tangled mess ensued. Sarai's disbelief and lack of trust led to the conception and birth of Ishmael, who later became the patriarch of the Islamic Nation.

The repercussions of a broken female relationship know no bounds, impacting more than we ever could imagine. I'm pretty sure Sarai had no idea of the generational impact her impatience with God's timing would produce.

These biblical examples of conflict do not show us how to resolve conflict; they simply show us that we live in a fallen world in which sin runs rampant, affecting relationships. So, how do you think Jesus wants us to respond to conflict?

Write an ending for each story that demonstrates a God-honoring way the relational conflict might have been addressed or resolved.

Jesus and the moneychangers, dove-sellers, and religious leaders in the Temple:

Sarai and Hagar:

> It's what we do *after* we sin that matters most.

If your endings involve humility on the part of Sarai and Hagar as well as the moneychangers and religious leaders, you're on to something, friend. With the exception of Jesus, everyone who has walked or now walks this earth is flesh-disabled—and there's no way around it until Jesus returns. No one is immune to sin. It's what we do *after* we sin that matters most.

If our hearts are hard and we refuse to humble ourselves, seeing our role in the conflict, then we cannot honor God with our post-sin actions. But when we humble ourselves before the Lord by asking Him to reveal our sin and trying to make things right with the other person, then we're honoring God.

If Sarai and Hagar had humbly admitted their sin to God and each other, forgiveness and perhaps reconciliation could have been possible. The same would have been true of the moneychangers, dove-sellers, and religious leaders in the Temple. The Gospels are clear that Jesus always offered grace and forgiveness whenever someone came to Him with a humble heart. Humility is so important to conflict resolution that we will be exploring it throughout the week.

None of us would argue that relational conflict is fun. Conflict is immensely stressful, horribly distracting, and emotionally draining; yet it can be the very thing that produces more authentic and God-honoring friendships! We'll begin learning how to walk through the steps of conflict resolution tomorrow, sweet friend.

Exhale. It will be good!

Turning to God

Ask God to reveal what He wants you to learn from the biblical examples of conflict we studied yesterday and today. What do you need to learn about conflict? The Holy Spirit will lead you in answering that question; in the meantime, ask God to give you the humility to see how you can better handle conflict. Thank Him for always being your source of peace and for giving you unending grace when you fall short.

DAY 3: USING THE P.E.G. SYSTEM TO WORK THROUGH CONFLICT

My heart was racing. With a furrowed brow and the feeling that the wind had been knocked out of my lungs, I hung up the phone and held on to the nearest chair. A woman I considered to be one of my closest friends had just unleashed a fury of words, and I felt as though I'd been sucker punched.

My immediate reaction to conflict is often to get on the phone right away with a trusted friend or my mother, explaining what happened and why I'm right and the other person is wrong. I feel as though I need to "enlist my team" so I can be reassured I'm in the right.

Can you say "pride"? Glory be!

The thing is, this isn't what God calls us to do when we're faced with a challenge, is it? God wants us to go to Him first.

God is the ultimate dispenser of wise counsel. When I'm experiencing conflict, first I need to pray and ask God to reveal my own sin. Then I need God's help to remove the log from my own eye and God's wisdom to handle the conflict in a manner that glorifies Him.

Read Psalm 111:10; Proverbs 3:13; and James 3:17. How would you define or describe wisdom? Why is it important for us to have it?

Now read James 1:5-8. What should we do if we lack wisdom and don't know what to do?

What does James say is the prerequisite for receiving wisdom?

> **Conflict is immensely stressful, horribly distracting, and emotionally draining; yet it can be the very thing that produces more authentic and God-honoring friendships!**

> **When we're stuck and can't budge, the Holy Spirit will provide the nudge.**

What does he say about those who doubt?

When we're stuck and can't budge, the Holy Spirit will provide the nudge. However, we first must believe that He is the one true God—not doubting it for a second.

The P.E.G. System is a three-step process intended to assist us in navigating relational conflict:

1. Pray
2. Examine
3. Go

Today we're going to focus on the first step, prayer. I don't know about you, but when I find myself in a tough situation, I just want to get out of it as soon as possible! However, instead of jumping on the phone to enlist my army, God wants me to turn to Him in prayer. This is what He wants each of us to do.

If I'm in the midst of a challenge, it's likely because I lack the wisdom I need to handle it. We must first go to the source Who provides the wisdom we need: God. I love my mother and I am blessed with a few wonderful and true Heart Sisters, but let's face it—none of them is God! While they are wise and can offer a biblical viewpoint, they're still human.

Sometimes I think we can get hung up on prayer—what to say, how to say it, whether or not it's OK to pray for certain situations to go in my favor. Of course, the answers will be different for different people, situations, and motives of the heart. But this I can say for certain: God wants us to talk to Him.

We can't have a relationship with someone we don't speak with on a regular basis. Prayer is simply talking to God. It doesn't have to be scripted. It doesn't have to be a memorized dictum. It doesn't have to be said in a specific tone, and it doesn't require certain words. It just needs to be spoken from our hearts.

Read 1 Kings 8:39 in the margin. What do we learn from this verse?

You know what is in everyone's heart. So from your home in heaven answer their prayers, according to the way they live and what is in their hearts.

(1 Kings 8:39 CEV)

God knows what's in our hearts. There isn't anything we can hide from Him. So, if God already knows what's in our hearts, why do we need to pray to Him?

Read Matthew 6:5-7.

In what way have the public-praying hypocrites already received their reward?

What does Jesus tell us we should do when we pray?

Scripture Challenge

To read more about biblical wisdom, check out these Scriptures: 2 Chronicles 1:8-11; Proverbs 4:6-7; 13:1; Colossians 2:2-3; James 1:5; 3:17.

This doesn't mean we shouldn't pray with friends or in a group, but there is no substitute for private, personal communion with God. Whenever and wherever we pray, we must always check the motives of our hearts. If our desire is to appear righteous or holy in front of everyone, then we have already received our reward. Though others may not be privy to the reality of what's in our hearts, God knows—every nook and cranny.

Now read Matthew 6:8 and complete the sentence below:

Your Father knows what you need before _____.

(NIV)

God knows our hearts and exactly what we need. He simply wants us to cry out to Him in humility and trust. We can't humble ourselves in our relationships with others if we cannot humble ourselves before God.

Nineteenth-century writer, teacher, and pastor Andrew Murray describes prayer this way: "Prayer is not monologue but dialogue; God's voice in response to mine is its most essential part."[2] In our busy world, it's easy to rattle off our list of desires and heartbreaks to God and then move on to the details of the day. Yet it's in our listening to God's response that we find the wisdom we need.

When I first heard this, I thought, "That's great. How do I hear Him?"

God speaks to us through Scripture, prayer, the Holy Spirit, other people, and the written and proclaimed word, including song. It's amazing what we'll hear when we slow down long enough to listen. That's part of our assignment today, sweet sister.

Fun Fact

Matthew 7:7 uses the verb *aiteo´*, which means "to ask for oneself."[3] This is different from a mere question; this is asking God *for* something. God wants us to ask Him for specifics.

Read the Scriptures below, and circle the one that most resonates with you:

*²⁸ Then they cried out to the L*ORD *in their trouble,*

and he brought them out of their distress.

²⁹ He stilled the storm to a whisper;

the waves of the sea were hushed.

³⁰ They were glad when it grew calm,

and he guided them to their desired haven.

(Psalm 107:28-30 NIV)

"If you believe, you will receive whatever you ask for in prayer."

(Matthew 21:22 NIV)

"Therefore I tell you, whatever you ask for in prayer, believe that you have received it, and it will be yours."

(Mark 11:24 NIV)

¹² "Very truly I tell you, whoever believes in me will do the works I have been doing, and they will do even greater things than these, because I am going to the Father. ¹³ And I will do whatever you ask in my name, so that the Father may be glorified in the Son. ¹⁴ You may ask me for anything in my name, and I will do it."

(John 14:12-14 NIV)

Why did you pick this particular passage? Write your thoughts below:

As I mentioned earlier, you don't have to follow a specific template or plan when praying; however, sometimes prayer methods can be helpful tools. One prayer method is the acrostic A.C.T.S. I have conversational prayer with God throughout the day; but when it comes to more focused prayer time, I often like to follow this method:

- **Adoration**: Give God praise and honor for who He is as Lord over all.
- **Confession**: Honestly talk about the sin in your life.
- **Thanksgiving**: Verbalize what you're grateful for in your own life and in the world around you.
- **Supplication**: Pray for the needs of others and yourself.

While I hope this gives you a framework for prayer when you need it, remember this: there is no "right" or "wrong" way to pray. Just pray! You don't need to say specific words or follow a certain format. God just wants you to reach out and communicate with Him. Though He knows what's in our hearts even before we speak, He wants us to open up and share it with Him. When we establish prayer time with God, we establish a relationship with God!

Turning to God

Find a comfy place where you can be quiet for at least ten minutes. You may choose to follow the A.C.T.S. process or just be in conversation with God. Regardless, give yourself time to listen. God may not respond to you right now; His answer might come later in the form of Scripture or song or a gentle nudge from the Holy Spirit. If you like, record your thoughts on the experience in the margin.

DAY 4: EXAMINE YOUR ROLE

Yesterday we discussed the importance of praying first when you become ensnared in a relational conflict. Today we're going to focus on the next step of the P.E.G. System: examine.

Allow me to share some ugly parts of my soul with you. (Now, isn't that just the most inspirational start to today's lesson?) When I find myself in relational conflict, sometimes I not only get on the phone and start to enlist people for Team Natalie but I also have been known to fail to see the error of my own ways in the situation.

Again, pride.

Though I'm making strides in this area, sometimes I still fail to stop and see the other person's perspective. When I'm more concerned with being right and justifying why the other person is wrong, I don't stop and examine my role with humility.

Yuck. So not the person I want to be—or the person God wants me to be.

Read Matthew 7:1-5 in the margin.

Summarize what Jesus is telling us in verses 1-2:

What are we to take out of our own eye, and why?

The Greek verb *krinete* is used for "judge" in verse 2, and in this context it means to pass censure—such as disapproval or condemnation.[4] It says that the consequence for judging harshly in this manner is that we will be judged in the same way. Ouch!

When it comes to specks and planks, we tend to think we have the speck and the other person has the plank. But Jesus says that when we're judging harshly, we have the plank! In order to examine ourselves accurately, we must see the situation with humility. As we've discussed previously, we can't humble ourselves before others if we can't humble ourselves before God? It's so true.

I once thought having humility meant that I didn't boast about myself. The end. Yet as I've matured in my relationship with God, I've learned it's about a whole lot more.

Think of humility as the opposite of pride. While pride says "Me, me, me!" humility says "You, you, you!" While pride is more concerned with appearances, humility is more concerned with the heart. While pride is about having a stiff, upper lip, humility is about having authentic and real relationships—junk and all.

If pride is the pretty front porch of your house, then humility is your dirty, messy living room. If your living room (or family room) looks like mine, there's a lot of junk strewn around! I would so much rather my relationships be rooted in humility than rooted in pride.

Read 1 Peter 5:6 in the margin. What are we to do, and what will God do in response?

It will be very difficult to humble ourselves in our relationships with others until we learn to humble ourselves in our relationship with God.

I admit that sometimes I formulate my plan and then run it by God so that I can keep Him in the loop, so to speak. That is pride, not humility. Humility consults with God first, asking for direction on what to do next. Humility recognizes that I am to be subordinate to God—that although His ways aren't my ways, He is the supreme, all-knowing, all-powerful, always-loving, mercy-giving, one true God. Running my plan by Him is out-of-order.

What else does God have to say about humility? Turns out, quite a bit! Let's look at just a small sample.

Write each verse or a summary in the chart below:

Proverbs 11:2	
Proverbs 22:4	
2 Chronicles 7:14	
Matthew 11:29-30	
James 4:10	

If pride is the pretty front porch of your house, then humility is your dirty, messy living room.

Scripture Challenge

One form of false humility is boasting (ironically) about your own humility—sometimes in sneaky ways, such as broadcasting sacrifices you have made. Check out these Scriptures on humility: Proverbs 16:19; Matthew 23:12; Philippians 2:3; Romans 12:3; 1 Peter 5:5-6; and James 4:10.

Proverbs 11:2 says that with humility comes wisdom. That's exactly what we're hoping to attain by following the P.E.G. System.

One of the most beautiful examples of humility in the Bible happened during the Last Supper. During the time of Jesus, people generally wore sandals or went barefoot. As a result, feet were extremely callused, often dirty, and...well...they smelled. So when guests entered a home, it was customary for the servant or the youngest child to wash the feet of their visitors.

Read John 13:1-17.

Who washed the disciples' feet?

Why do you think Peter reacted the way he did?

Why did Jesus wash the disciples' feet?

What did He ask them to do?

How can we figuratively wash one another's feet?

No one, not even Jesus, is above serving another. If we are to have a mind-set of serving and loving others as Jesus commanded, then we also must strive to see their point of view when conflicts arise.

When those conflicts do arise—as they inevitably will—there are five questions we can ask ourselves to determine if we need to speak to the one who has hurt us.

1. What is my role in this conflict?

Read Psalm 139:23-24, and write the verses below or summarize their meaning.

Like it or not, even the most innocent party in a conflict can still play a role in the disagreement. A long time ago, a friend of mine was hurt by my actions, which she perceived to be against her. The truth of the matter was that it had been an emotional twenty-four hours for me, and I was running on two hours of sleep. In prayer the following morning (while in the shower, of all places!), it was evident to me that I needed to go to her and apologize for what I had done, which had not been intended to hurt her. Though it wasn't received in the manner I had hoped it would be, that's all right because it was about my obedience to God.

When we follow through in obedience, we do our part before the Lord. God has His own thing going on with the other person. We can't control how someone will react to our humility. As we'll learn next week, sometimes we have to accept someone else's unforgiveness, because we can't *make* them forgive us. (Though we always can forgive ourselves.) It's important to remember that we can't change someone else—only the Holy Spirit has the power to do that.

2. Am I hurt because of my own insecurity?

Read Matthew 7:24-27, and draw or write your interpretation of these verses below:

If we build our house on the sand, it will eventually give way to the elements. The same is true of insecurity—if we don't root our identity in who God says we are, then eventually we'll be shaken.

So often I have reacted to others negatively because I felt guilty of something I had failed to do, and deep down I knew that I was wrong. We should always ask ourselves, "Is there a trigger from my own brokenness that this friend has unknowingly set off? Is this more of a 'me' thing than a 'her' thing?" If so, then it's possible we're hurt because of our own insecurity, not because of something another person has said or done.

3. Am I expecting too much from this relationship? Has this friendship become an idol?

Read 1 John 2:15-17 in the margin. In one sentence, write what you think is the main idea of these verses:

[15] Do not love this world nor the things it offers you, for when you love the world, you do not have the love of the Father in you. [16] For the world offers only a craving for physical pleasure, a craving for everything we see, and pride in our achievements and possessions. These are not from the Father, but are from this world. [17] And this world is fading away, along with everything that people crave. But anyone who does what pleases God will live forever.

(1 John 2:15-17)

> There's a God-shaped hole in all of us, and often we expect it to be filled by our sideways relationships rather than our vertical relationship with God.

I'm no stranger to making my relationships an idol. Here's the deal: there's a God-shaped hole in all of us, and often we expect it to be filled by our sideways relationships with others rather than our vertical relationship with God. The reason so many people flit from relationship to relationship is because no one can fill that God-shaped hole—only God can. If you are expecting too much from a friend, she will eventually feel the pressure and start to back off. And in case you're wondering, your husband or significant other will, too.

This is why getting right with God is a must if you desire healthy relationships. Is there a friend you expect to make you her number one priority—even over God and her family? Do you make her feel guilty if she chooses to stay home and watch TV instead of going out with you because she just needs a little down time? Do you expect hour-long chat sessions when she is in an extremely busy season of work or family life? Our own emotional baggage should not dictate the expectations and overall tone of our friendships because no one can be our everything. Only God can!

4. Will I be able to spend time with this person without feeling hurt or resentful?

Read Ephesians 4:25-26 in the margin. What does God want us to do with one another? Why?

What are we cautioned to not do?

> 25 So stop telling lies. Let us tell our neighbors the truth, for we are all parts of the same body. 26 And "don't sin by letting anger control you." Don't let the sun go down while you are still angry.
>
> (Ephesians 4:25-26)

Confession: I can lose my cool sometimes. (You are learning some lovely things about me, aren't you? Just being honest.) The thing is, when I'm angry—regardless of whether that anger is of the righteous kind or not—I sometimes say and do things I'm not proud of later. But God's Word says that in our anger, we are not to sin. I should probably tattoo that to my forehead!

If a friend has hurt you and you feel that failing to address this hurt will force you to overreact to every little flaw in your friend, or if your guard is always up when you're with her, then you probably need to discuss the issue with her.

5. Can I trust this person and be vulnerable with her?

Read John 8:32 in the margin. What does the truth do for us?

"And you will know the truth, and the truth will set you free."

(John 8:32)

Authenticity is a buzzword these days. We live in a culture that values the real and eschews the false, which is good. If you're unwilling to go deep, surface friendships you will reap. If you won't allow a friend past your pretty front porch and invite her into your messy living room, you're simply going to have a surface friendship. Although John 8:32 is talking about the truth of God's Word, truth in general provides more freedom than the chains of secrets.

If you can't be your true self with your friends, then it's probably time to reevaluate your friendships. If you can't be truthful with those who love you, then maybe you need to assess if that love is an authentic love for your well-being or just a love of convenience. If you constantly are worrying about saying the wrong thing or wondering if you can trust someone, then the weight of those chains eventually will become exhausting and you will lose the freedom that comes with truth.

The truth will set us free, and this is the truth: life on earth is too short to live outside of anything less than freedom!

If you're unwilling to go deep, surface friendships you will reap.

Turning to God

I encourage you to take at least ten minutes to just sit quietly with God, as you did yesterday. Ask Him the following questions, and then pause for a moment to hear His answers. Though the answers may not come right away, it's a good practice to pause and listen—because sometimes they do! You can write your responses or simply reflect.

What relationships are working well in my life? Why are they working well?

What relationships are not working well in my life? Why not? What's my role in this?

If you can't be your true self with your friends, then it's probably time to reevaluate your friendships.

What are two things I can do today to improve my relationships with others?

Most important, how can I improve my relationship with God?

DAY 5: GO SPEAK THE TRUTH IN LOVE

This week we've been exploring the P.E.G. System for addressing relational conflict. We've seen that first we need to go to God in prayer, and then we should examine our role in the conflict. The third step is to go to the other person who has hurt us (or whom we have hurt) and talk it through. Before we dive into this final step, I'd like to say a preliminary word about seeking counsel, which sometimes can be helpful preparation for this final step.

There are times when, in order to be ready to go to the other person, I need to seek wise counsel from a trusted sister in Christ. However, talking with someone outside the conflict can be a slippery slope that easily turns into a gossip train if we aren't very careful. So it is critical that we are both intentional and wise when selecting this individual. Depending on the situation, sometimes it can be better to select someone who does not know the other individual(s) involved—or to speak with a pastor.

The purpose of wise counsel is to assist us in identifying our sin in a given situation and to provide valuable insights we otherwise might not see when our emotions are strong. Let's see what the Bible says about seeking wise counsel.

What does each of the following Proverbs say about seeking wise counsel?

Proverbs 1:5

Proverbs 12:26

Proverbs 15:22

Proverbs 15:31

Clearly it isn't a bad thing to seek wise counsel when needed. In fact, it can be prudent to seek the advice of those who are qualified to give it when we are unsure of how to handle a matter. C. S. Lewis once said, "The next best thing to be being wise oneself is to live in a circle of those who are."[5]

Those qualified to give wise counsel are people who are:

- knowledgeable about the Word of God,
- experienced in handling conflict or relationships in general,
- willing to speak the truth in love,
- able to apply Scripture to their lives, and
- compassionate and possess a strong sense of integrity.

While there is a time and place to seek wise counsel, attempting to enlist support as we bad-mouth the other person is *not* seeking wise counsel. That's considered gossip, and the Scriptures are clear that God isn't fond of gossip. Besides, when we gossip, we show our listeners that we might someday gossip about them as well.

> **Have you ever made an attempt to seek wise counsel that resulted in gossip? What happened to your relationship with the other person(s) involved in the conflict?**

> **When has seeking wise counsel been a positive and helpful experience for you?**

Now that we've addressed wise counsel, let's dive into step three, "Go," by revisiting Sarai and Hagar's story, which we read on Day 2.

> **It's OK for friends to disagree, but a true Heart Sister is one who won't flee. She'll stick it out and talk it out.**

According to Genesis 16:6, why did Hagar leave?

It's tempting to flee the scene when we're hurting, isn't it? Sometimes the pain can be so severe that we just want to take matters into our own hands and do something—anything—that will relieve us of the sting.

It's our natural inclination to get out of uncomfortable situations as quickly as possible because, truthfully, it's easier simply not to deal with it. Sometimes it is, indeed, easier to walk away from a relationship that has become difficult. But here's the thing: eventually there will be some kind of conflict in *every single one* of our deeper relationships. The only way to ensure that your relationships won't have conflict is to keep them on a surface level. If you have only surface-level friendships, you won't have to risk the threat of relational conflict—but you'll be a very lonely woman!

Review Genesis 16:9-10. What did the angel of the Lord tell Hagar to do, and how would she be rewarded if she did this?

I think this is one of the greatest examples in the Bible of someone who felt the urge to "go" back to someone after a conflict. It is not noted in the text what was said between the two women upon Hagar's return, but I'm certain *something* was said.

When a person has the courage to walk through conflict with a friend, she too can be rewarded. She can be rewarded with a friend who knows her more intimately and who is willing to listen to her heart with humility and grace. And that makes for a deeper friendship!

It's true that many choose to follow their initial reaction to flee when relationships get difficult, yet in doing so they miss the potential fruit of reconciliation. It's OK for friends to disagree, but a true Heart Sister is one who won't flee. She'll stick it out and talk it out.

Read Matthew 18:15 in the margin. What are we told to do when someone has offended us?

"If another believer sins against you, go privately and point out the offense. If the other person listens and confesses it, you have won that person back."

(Matthew 18:15)

Jesus was clear that we are to "go" and speak to the persons who have hurt us. But why?

Read Matthew 5:23-24.

"Therefore, if you are offering your gift at the _____

and there remember that your brother or sister has something against

you, leave your gift there in front of the altar. First _____ and

be _____ to them; then come and offer your

_____." (NIV)

These verses tell us to interrupt our worship if there is someone who might be disgruntled with us or if we have unaddressed relational discord with anyone. We are simply to "go." If we choose not to "go," that unresolved conflict will become a barrier to our worship of God, which eventually leads to a barrier in our relationship with God in general.

Isn't that precisely what Jesus did for us? Sin entered the world and broke our relationship with God. Jesus was without fault—He didn't eat the apple, choosing His own way instead of God's way. Yet God told Him to "go"—to take the initiative to restore relationship with us, to choose relationship at all costs, and to do all He could to live in peace among everyone. Jesus makes us friends with God because He was willing to go when God told Him to go. Jesus was innocent, but God told Him to finish it and make it right; and He did.

I'll be straight with you. I don't always want to "go." I've mentioned that I don't really like conflict. It's far easier in the short run to sweep it under the rug and move on. But if I have examined the situation through the five questions we discussed yesterday and have determined I need to speak to the person who hurt me, then I'm being disobedient if I don't do it. I want to be obedient to God, but my plans can be derailed by avoidance and pride. It's difficult to release our pride and admit our mistakes in humility, but you want to know what's worse? Not obeying God's command.

Pride is a sneaky sin that grips us all at some point. Turns out, being prideful is more than just boasting. It's about not accepting help when you really need it because "you've got it all under control." It's about refusing to see your sin in a given situation, so you refuse to seek reconciliation because it's clearly "her fault." It's about refusing to forgive. It's about not admitting you've struggled with something. It's refusing even to attempt reconciliation in a broken relationship.

Scripture Challenge

Humility is a predominant theme in the Scriptures! For more insights and examples of this Christlike characteristic, see Genesis 18:27; Exodus 3:11; Joshua 7:6; 2 Chronicles 32:26, 34:27; Job 42:6; Psalm 25:9; Isaiah 6:5; Matthew 8:8; Mark 10:45; Luke 5:8; and 1 Peter 5:5.

Throughout the week we have discussed humility, because it's that important to conflict resolution. Being humble during a conflict means being willing to go to the other person involved in a non-accusatory manner while owning our part, asking for forgiveness, and moving toward reconciliation. A lack of humility, on the other hand, might sound something like this:

- "What are you so uptight about?"
- "I know you can't be mad at me because I didn't do anything wrong, so what's bothering you?"
- "OK," "Whatever," "Fine" (or any other generic phrase that neither accepts the other person's apology nor admits any wrongdoing).
- "I accept your apology" (without admitting your own role in the conflict, regardless of who did "more" to hurt the other).

During the two years I led a large women's ministry program, I observed that humility was the determining factor in whether a friendship would last. Friends who were able to go to one another with humble hearts by owning her part, seeking to reconcile, and choosing relationship instead of strife were the ones who actually entered a deeper level of intimacy with one another and became Heart Sisters. The relationships that disintegrated were almost always due to a complete lack of humility—either on both sides or just one. As a matter of fact, this is true of all relationships—not just friendships. Humility is the foundation of all safe and healthy relationships. The five most powerful words are "I'm sorry. I was wrong."

John the Baptist provides a wonderful example of humility in the way that he responded when Jesus' ministry began to grow.

Read John 3:25-30 and complete verse 30 below:

"He must become _____; I must become _____." (NIV)

Humility is the key that unlocks hearts.

John knew that the focus needed to be on Jesus and His ministry, not himself. That is true for us, as well. God cannot increase in us unless we humble ourselves. If we want more of God, we must think less about ourselves. And as we've discussed, this humility in our relationship with the Lord spills over into our relationships with others. Humility is the key that unlocks hearts.

Besides making sure that our hearts are humble when we "go," we also must be willing to keep the best interests of the other person at the forefront while speaking the truth in love. The Apostle Paul tells us why we are to speak the truth in love.

According to Ephesians 4:15 (in the margin), why are we to speak the truth in love?

Instead, we will speak the truth in love, growing in every way more and more like Christ, who is the head of his body, the church.

(Ephesians 4:15)

The following verses give us some clues about what it means to speak the truth in love. Read and summarize each one. Then place a star next to the one that speaks to you the most.

Ephesians 4:29

Romans 12:18

Proverbs 15:1

1 Corinthians 16:14

1 Peter 5:3

Though speaking the truth in love is something we are to do in situations of strife, we should *always* speak the truth in love. Will we sometimes forget to do this? Absolutely. Thank God for grace. Literally.

A couple of months ago, I could sense that something was "off" in one of my friendships. I wasn't sure what it was because I couldn't think of anything I had done, but yet I was bothered by the distance and wondered if I had hurt my friend in some way.

I'm guessing maybe you've experienced something like that as well. Maybe you've had a friend who stopped calling you back or quit returning your texts. Maybe she's always "busy" when you ask her to get together for lunch.

If you notice this kind of change in a relationship, then I would advise you to go to your friend and ask: "Have I hurt or offended you in any way?"

I don't think we do this enough, sisters. I truly believe that sometimes we allow friendships to fade because we're too scared to ask this critical question—a question that could help to clear up a misunderstanding and result in a closer friendship.

Have you ever asked a friend this question? If so, what happened?

Of course, not all discussions end with a closer friendship—even when we speak the truth in love. Perhaps you've had that experience. Unfortunately, I have too. We'll talk about that next week...

Turning to God

Conflict is never easy—and that includes thinking about it. But we've done some important work this week. I think you've earned a long nap, a bubble bath, or some chocolate (or perhaps all three)! Be good to yourself when you're doing deep work like this, sweet sister. God strips us of our layers when we're ready to shed them, but it isn't necessarily pain free. Yet with the pain of this inner work comes the most beautiful exterior fruit. Learning how to resolve conflict helps us to cultivate the fruit of authentic friendships.

Take a moment and thank God for loving you the way He does. Thank Him for His gentleness. Thank Him for His truth, compassion, and new mercies. Next, ask Him to help you cultivate a spirit of humility—in your relationship with Him and your relationships with others. Then go be good to yourself!

CLASH OF THE TITANS

If it is possible, as far as it depends on you, live at peace with everyone.
(Romans 12:18 NIV)

Pace maker go after peace; *Peace taker* steal peace.

When we are no longer afraid of *conflict*, we are no longer afraid of *relationships* because we are equipped to handle whatever comes our way.

The first step of the P.E.G. system is to *pray*.

Ask God to do four things:

1. *reveal* your sin in the situation.
2. *direct* you on when to speak to who has hurt you.
3. *provide* the opportunity to do so.
4. *prepare* both of your hearts so both sides can be humble and not proud.

"Call to me and I will answer you and tell you great and unsearchable things you do not know."

(Jeremiah 33:3 NIV)

God wants us to go to Him *first*, even though He already knows what's *troubling* us.

The next step of the P.E.G. System is to *examine* your role in the conflict.

VIDEO VIEWER GUIDE: WEEK 3

5 Questions to Ask Yourself

1. What is my ___role___ in this conflict?

2. Am I hurt because of my own ___insecurity___?

3. Am I expecting too much from this relationship? Has this friendship become an ___idol___?

4. Will I be able to spend time with this person without feeling ___hurt___ or resentful?

5. Can I ___trust___ this person and be vulnerable with her? ___Real authentic___

The third step in the P.E.G. system is to ___Go___.

David, Ziba, and Mephibosheth

Part 1: see 2 Samuel 16:1-4

Part 2:

24 Mephibosheth, Saul's grandson, also went down to meet the king. He had not taken care of his feet or trimmed his mustache or washed his clothes from the day the king left until the day he returned safely. 25 When he came from Jerusalem to meet the king, the king asked him, "Why didn't you go with me, Mephibosheth?"

26 He said, "My lord the king, since I your servant am lame, I said, 'I will have my donkey saddled and will ride on it, so I can go with the king.' But Ziba my servant betrayed me. 27 And he has slandered your servant to my lord the king. My lord the king is like an angel of God; so do whatever you wish. 28 All my grandfather's descendants deserved nothing but death from my lord the king, but you gave your servant a place among those who eat at your table. So what right do I have to make any more appeals to the king?"

VIDEO VIEWER GUIDE: WEEK 3

²⁹ The king said to him, "Why say more? I order you and Ziba to divide the land."

³⁰ Mephibosheth said to the king, "Let him take everything, now that my lord the king has returned home safely."

(2 Samuel 19:24-30 NIV)

Unless we "go," we cannot know the other person's ___true___ ___intentions___.

If God calls us to go and speak to someone who has hurt us, He expects us to speak the ___truth___ in ___love___.

Both parties must also value the ___relationship___ more than being ___right___.

Week 4

THE FORGIVENESS BUSINESS

LETTING GO AND BEING FREE

Memory Verse

Bear with each other and forgive one another if any of you has a grievance against someone. Forgive as the Lord forgave you. And over all these virtues put on love, which binds them all together in perfect unity.

(Colossians 3:13-14 NIV)

Just Between Us

On October 2, 2006, Charlie Roberts, a Lancaster County deliveryman, burst into a one-room Amish schoolhouse in Nickel Mines, Pennsylvania, carrying a shotgun and various restraining devices. He ordered the teacher and all male students to leave. He then proceeded to restrain ten young girls, and eventually he shot each child. Roberts then ended his own life. Five of the girls were killed; the other five were very seriously injured.[1]

Tragically, stories such as this are becoming far more commonplace these days. It seems that every time I turn on the news or read a newspaper, there are stories that make me wring my hands and plead with Jesus to just come back. Today.

But what's different about this particular tragedy is that several members of the Amish community visited Charlie Roberts's parents and widow just hours after he killed five of their young girls. They insisted the family remain in Lancaster County. They expressed their forgiveness. They provided food and prayer. They even attended Roberts's funeral. Yes. Let that sink in: they attended the funeral of the man who killed five of their young girls.

Can you even imagine? I don't know about you, but forgiveness has been quite a journey for me. I'm typically not one who can immediately forgive; it takes time for my heart to move into a posture of forgiveness.

Maybe you're like me, too. Maybe you're thinking, "That's amazing, Natalie. But I'm not Amish. I was dealt a raw deal. I was mistreated. Abused. Betrayed. I can't forgive that easily."

I get it. Oh, boy, do I ever. I'm so, so sorry for your hurt. But here's the thing: forgiveness isn't for the offender's benefit; it's for *our* benefit.

As we'll discover this week, an unforgiving heart will lead to bitterness, anger, and resentment. Our memory verse also explains that we are to forgive others because the Lord has forgiven *us*.

I've been granted far more grace than I deserve. My guess is that you have as well. Forgiveness will allow us to release the weight we carry from past hurts *and* please God.

Sounds good to me. What about you?

DAY 1: WHY DO WE NEED TO FORGIVE?

Lately I've been reflecting on my own ragged journey with forgiveness in the past. I recall a time when I was struggling to forgive (we've all been there, right?). A dear friend called to ask how I was feeling about a hurtful situation that had happened with one of my other friends. "I will forgive her when she asks for it!" I declared. "She doesn't deserve my forgiveness, and I certainly won't give it to her without being asked. I can't just let her get by with this!" (Oh, sister, do you hear the pride in my attitude?) My friend on the other end of the line, who probably was regretting her unfortunate timing, listened patiently, knowing it wasn't the right moment for a rebuke. That's one wise friend, right?

Unfortunately, for a long time I believed the lie that forgiveness must be deserved or requested. There was so much I didn't understand about the process of forgiveness—and believe me, forgiveness is a process.

When I was a young girl, my father struggled with alcoholism. In fact, he didn't stop drinking until I was twenty-two years old. As a result, he floated in and out of my life. If he was sober for a period of time, he was in. If he was drinking, he was out. I grew up believing that I wasn't important enough for my father to stop drinking. Although I now understand that was not true, children do not typically understand the behavior of addicts. Unfortunately, children are keen observers but lousy interpreters.

Turning to food in my pain, I became a chubby little girl, and it hurt when others teased me for being plump. When my body began to change during puberty, that extra weight shifted, and the boys began to notice—particularly older boys. Unfortunately, the older girls didn't like that, and I became a target of bullying. Throughout my teen years, I was told I wasn't skinny enough, pretty enough, smart enough, popular enough—you-name-it enough. In time I began to believe the naysayers, thinking I just wasn't enough of anything.

In college I met the man I would eventually marry—a man who, like my father, struggled with addictions. We were divorced after just eighteen months. It was during the time of my divorce that I became a follower of Jesus. I remember one warm, spring day sobbing in my living room as I asked God why everything was so difficult for me while so many other people seemed to pass through life unscathed. Through His gentle nudging, I realized that although I had been *a* victim, I no longer had to be *the* victim.

I certainly had quite a few people to forgive: my father, the girls who had bullied me, the people who had said and done hurtful things, my ex-husband. What I didn't understand on that spring day and didn't fully understand until many years later is that forgiveness is not for the other person. It's for me—and it's for you.

There was something else I did not fully understand about forgiveness.

Read Matthew 6:14-15. What happens when we forgive others? What happens when we don't?

[14] "For if you forgive other people when they sin against you, your heavenly Father will also forgive you. [15] But if you do not forgive others their sins, your Father will not forgive your sins."
(Matthew 6:14-15 NIV)

Jesus' message is clear. Our lack of forgiveness for others results in our own lack of forgiveness from God. Does that make you as hot under the collar as it does me? The good news is that our loving God is full of mercy and grace and freely forgives a repentant heart!

Do you feel like you just need to pause right now and talk to God about any unforgiveness in your heart? If so, go right ahead. What do you hear God saying to you?

Forgiveness is the number one stumbling block we face when it comes to relationships, because it's simply not in our human nature to love someone who has hurt or offended us. Our flesh cries out for us to get even when we are at odds with someone else. We're often encouraged to settle the score because we live in a culture where many believe "an eye for an eye" is still a justifiable reaction when someone hurts us. When we feel rejected, we often revert to self-preservation mode, wanting to protect ourselves at all costs—except that's not the way of Jesus. Having the humility of Jesus means we care about valuing and choosing relationship rather than being right or getting even.

Some of you, like me, have been through some really hard stuff. Maybe someone you once trusted abused you. Maybe you were falsely accused of something that changed the trajectory of your life. Maybe you were rejected or abandoned by a parent or husband. Maybe a child has turned away from

Having the humility of Jesus means we care about valuing and choosing relationship rather than being right or getting even.

the faith you so diligently tried to imprint in his or her heart. The pain is real, and Jesus cares about it all. Yet He calls us to forgive it *all*—every single offense, big and small—because that's how He forgives us!

But if we confess our sins to him, he is faithful and just to forgive us our sins and to cleanse us from all wickedness.

(1 John 1:9)

Look again at 1 John 1:9 (in the margin), which we read last week. When we confess our sins, what does God do? Complete the sentence below:

He will forgive our _____ and cleanse us from _____ wickedness.

One of my favorite moments of forgiveness in the Bible involves David and Saul. Before we dive into that story tomorrow, we need to know the backstory.

Read 1 Samuel 18:6-9. In one or two sentences, describe what happened. How did Saul feel about David after this?

Fun Fact

Because David was not serving in the army with his brothers at the time he fought Goliath, it is thought that he was less than twenty years old—the age when men could serve in the army of Israel (see Numbers 1:3).

Saul's pride led to jealousy. Though we talked about bone-rotting envy last week, it's worth highlighting again here because jealousy is often an underlying factor in broken relationships—and consequently an obstacle to forgiveness. So I encourage you to lean in with attentive ears as we explore this part of the backstory.

It's easy to read this passage and think, *Well, that Saul! He was so prideful and jealous! How could he allow his brokenness to be projected on an innocent boy?* Yet if we're honest, we've all allowed pride and jealousy to negatively influence our opinions of others. No doubt we've also been on the receiving end of others' jealousy.

Unfortunately, there are people in this world who may not like you just because you're you. Maybe your light shines too brightly on their darkness. Maybe you excel at something they dream to do. Maybe they take your success personally, as if you are successful to spite them, instead of rejoicing over your achievements with you. The green-eyed monster of our jealousy can lead us to say and do some pretty ugly things, and Saul was no exception.

Now read 1 Samuel 19:1-12. Create a flow chart of the key events in these passages by answering the following questions.

What did Saul want to do initially? Who talked him out of it?

_____

_____

⬇

Saul backed off for a while, but then what happened to arouse his jealousy again? What did Saul try to do?

_____

_____

⬇

What did David do in response?

_____

_____

⬇

What did Michal encourage David to do, and how did David respond?

_____

_____

Saul literally wanted to kill David because he was jealous of David's success. If we read further in First Samuel, we learn that this was the moment when Saul embarked on a four-year attempt to capture and kill David.

Even though we've probably never been on a murderous rampage like Saul, jealousy can wreak havoc in our hearts and souls. As we close today, let's take a moment for an honest inventory.

Scripture Challenge

Jealousy is often at the root of relational conflict, and in the Scriptures we see the damaging effects this can have not only in the lives of individuals and families but also in the life of the church. Trace the effects of envy in these biblical examples: Genesis 4; 37; Matthew 20:1-16; Luke 15:11-31; Acts 13:44-52.

Recall a time when you were jealous of someone. How did your jealousy affect your thoughts, words, and actions? How did it affect your life?

Is there any jealousy in your heart now? If so, how is it affecting your life?

If jealousy were abolished from your life forever, how would that affect any broken relationships where forgiveness is needed?

If jealousy were eliminated, God would be vindicated. You see, jealousy leads to relational strife; so if relational strife didn't exist, relationships would be restored and protected. The evil one desires to derail us through relational conflict, but if we don't allow it and choose instead to live a life without jealousy, well, then, God is vindicated. Sweet victory, indeed!

Turning to God

Spend some time with the ultimate relationship healer. Find a place where you can be without distractions for at least five minutes (or longer if possible). Ask God to search your heart and reveal any broken or strained relationships where your own jealousy is a factor. Confess your jealousy to God and ask Him to release you from it. Pray for the person or persons involved, asking God to bless them with His favor, love, and grace. Pray that God will give you a pure heart and help you identify when feelings of jealousy are beginning to surface. Close your time thanking God for His gentle grace, and then embrace that grace. It's a beautiful thing!

Depending on your situation and personal struggle, you may have to repeat this process in the days to come. Just as forgiveness is not a "one and done" thing, neither are our struggles that contribute to broken relationships.

DAY 2: CASTING OFF RESENTMENT, BITTERNESS, AND ANGER

Several years ago, my husband and I were in a small group that went very awry. Hurt feelings and deep wounds resulted, and everyone was left wondering what on earth went wrong. The church we attended wasn't sure how to handle the situation, and this created another level of hurt in our already smarting hearts. We were dealing with both relational pain and church pain. It was a rough season, friend. I found myself retreating from others out of fear that I would be hurt again.

After the drama we had experienced, I thought it would be better to have just a few trustworthy friends and my family. No need to put myself out there much; that was too risky and just plain scary. My husband and I also began to resent those who had caused the conflict, leading to our own bitterness and anger. After confessing this to God one fall afternoon, He revealed a very powerful truth to me: refusing to forgive only hurts you, because the by-products of unforgiveness are resentment, bitterness, and anger.

Doesn't sound like much fun, does it?

Have you ever tasted a rotten piece of fruit? The bitter taste overpowers our taste buds, and we can't spit it out fast enough. Similarly, bitterness leaves a rotten taste in our mouths and our souls. Author Anne Lamott says it like this: "Not forgiving is like drinking rat poison and then waiting for the rat to die."[2] When we wait for the rat to die, we're silently killing ourselves—and we don't even know it.

Read Hebrews 12:15 in the margin. What happens when bitterness takes root in us?

Look after each other so that none of you fails to receive the grace of God. Watch out that no poisonous root of bitterness grows up to trouble you, corrupting many.
(Hebrews 12:15)

How would you describe a bitter person?

Has there been a time in your own life when this description fit you? If so, what was the cause of your bitterness?

No one is born bitter. We become bitter through life experiences. We've all heard the cliché "It can make you bitter or better." It's a cliché for a reason: it's truth.

We can indeed choose to be bitter or better, even when it's not a conscious choice. If we are feeling bitter, it's probably because we are resenting someone for something. According to Merriam-Webster's New Collegiate Dictionary, the word *resentment* means "a feeling of indignant displeasure or persistent ill will at something regarded as a wrong, insult, or injury."[3] So when we are resentful and bitter, there is something we are not forgiving.

Read Ephesians 4:31. What things are we to rid ourselves of according to Paul?

What are we to do instead?

There is a reason Paul gave these instructions. Resentment, bitterness, and anger are like battery acid to the soul, eating us alive.

Yesterday we learned the backstory for one of my favorite stories of forgiveness in the Bible. We saw that Saul was jealous of David and wanted to kill him. When David ran, Saul ran after him—and continued chasing him for four years. Now that was one bitter man! Now we come to the point in the story where we witness the power of forgiveness.

This story of forgiveness may not be what you were expecting. There is no beautiful moment between David and Saul. Tragically, Saul took his own life in battle, and his sons were killed as well. Yet what is surprising is how David, Saul's nemesis, reacted.

Read 2 Samuel 1:11-12. How did David react to the news of Saul's and Jonathan's deaths?

> Resentment, bitterness, and anger are like battery acid to the soul, eating us alive.

During Old Testament days, the tearing of clothing and fasting were common ways to show intense grief and mourning for the dead. After all the turmoil he had suffered at the hands of Saul, David still showed grief and respect by tearing his clothes and refusing food and drink. Can you imagine?

Our world tells us we should rejoice if our enemies are struck down, and sometimes we believe the lie that revenge really is the best medicine. Though I wouldn't rejoice over the death of anyone, I wouldn't necessarily be overcome with grief upon hearing of the death of someone who wanted to kill me. Yet this is the picture of David we see here.

Now read 2 Samuel 9. What did David ask in verse 1?

Who was presented to David, and what was his relationship to Saul and Jonathan?

What did David do for him?

Not only did David mourn Saul's and Jonathan's deaths, he honored Jonathan's son by offering a place at his table. It's true that Jonathan was a loyal friend to David despite his father's anger and jealousy. However, David still chose to protect the lineage of Saul by caring for Jonathan's son, Mephibosheth, even though he was under no obligation to do so. Only a heart free from all bitterness—a forgiving heart—would have been able to do that.

David had every reason to be angry, resentful, and bitter toward Saul. For crying out loud, the poor boy didn't do a single thing to warrant a death threat! Yet David didn't waste his time on those negative, destructive emotions. Instead, he chose to forgive.

Many of the psalms were written by David when he was being chased by Saul through Israel, and they show us that he chose to cry out to God rather than to people. They also show us that he trusted God to take care of him no matter what. David seemed to believe that even though he suffered, God had a plan for him—and it was a good one.

Review the description of a bitter person you wrote on page 115. Then compare and contrast that person with David by completing the Venn diagram below.

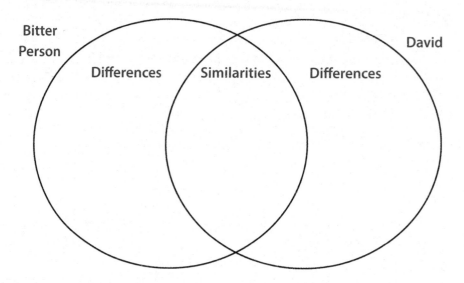

Bitter Person   Differences   Similarities   Differences   **David**

Suffering usually involves the need for forgiveness, because much of our suffering involves other people.

I hope you noted in the area of similarities that David and the bitter person both experienced suffering. In John 16:33, we read that Jesus said we will have trouble in this world. He didn't say we *might* have trouble; he said we *will*.

We aren't guaranteed an easy ride. We will suffer at some point during our lives. And here's the thing: suffering usually involves the need for forgiveness, because much of our suffering involves other people.

Let's close our time today with some hope, shall we? While suffering is inevitable, there is good that comes from our trials.

Read 1 Peter 4:12-19 and answer the following.

Why are we not to be surprised by trials?

Why can we rejoice in trials?

Why are we blessed if we are insulted for the name of Christ?

What are we to do when we suffer as a Christian?

If we are suffering in a manner that pleases God, what are we to continue doing?

When we forgive and let go of the heavy burdens of anger, resentment, and bitterness, we are better able to walk in the freedom God wants us to experience. The best way to walk lighter, move more freely, and become our true selves is to forgive. And forgive again. Rinse and repeat.

Read Matthew 18:21-22. What did Peter ask, and what was Jesus' answer?

I just have to say it: sometimes Peter makes me giggle. I identify with him so much! His pride was exhibited here because many scholars believe he was trying to impress Jesus—sort of like, "Look how much I understand your teachings, Jesus!" Peter thought seven times would be an exorbitant amount of times to forgive someone. However, Jesus multiplied that number to prove His point: we are to forgive a limitless amount of times. As we'll learn next week, that doesn't mean you repeatedly allow yourself to be mistreated. Instead, it means that you will no longer allow other people's actions and treatment of you to decay your heart and soul through unforgiveness. That's an important lesson we all need to learn.

Turning to God

Several years ago, I took part in a ministry that focused on ridding yourself of hurtful offenses that had transpired in your past. Honestly, I didn't think I was holding on to much from my past, but my participation in this ministry revealed that I was. The leaders instructed me to end each day by asking God to reveal whom I needed to forgive—either from my past or just from that day. After God revealed those I needed to release, I was to pray these words:

"Father, I forgive _____ for _____.
Please bless him/her today so that he/she can feel your love."

Today I invite you to do the same. Find a quiet place and ask God whom you need to forgive. Then, forgive them and bless them.

Remember that forgiveness is not a "one and done" thing, nor is it condoning someone else's sin or poor treatment of you. You might have to forgive the same person for the same offense every day for a while. Be patient with the process and embrace the grace, friend. I'm praying for your freedom.

DAY 3: MODELING FORGIVENESS TO AN UNFORGIVING WORLD

See if you can quickly complete these common sayings:

An eye for an _____.

Don't get mad, get _____.

_____ revenge.

An eye for an eye. Don't get mad, get even. Sweet revenge. That was easy, right? These sayings reflect the mind-set of our culture in which unforgiveness is the accepted norm. As Christians, we know we are called to forgive, but it can be a difficult process. Sometimes it can seem *impossible*.

Thirty years ago my friend Rhonda was standing in her kitchen preparing for a Memorial Day weekend barbecue and a houseful of guests. Her nine-year-old son, Jake, ran in to see her, proudly showed off his new shirt, gave her a hug, and bounded out the door. Moments later, while riding his bike with his older sister, Jake was killed by a drunk driver. One person's poor choice cost this sweet boy his life—and broke his mother's heart.

Immediately after hitting Jake, the driver was seen throwing beer cans out of his truck. Rhonda said, "I was so angry at this man because not only did he kill my son but he also showed no remorse. He wasn't concerned about how Jake was; he was concerned only about himself."

Rhonda was angry for quite some time. Unfortunately, some Christians in her community said unhelpful things like, "You need to forgive and move on." Rhonda shared with me, "I knew that, but it's not what I needed to hear at that given moment. I needed to hear that was OK to feel angry—it just wasn't OK to stay angry forever."

"I wanted this man who killed my son to hurt like I hurt," Rhonda added. "I was bitter and miserable. I knew God never left me; my bitterness, anger, and resentment caused me to leave Him."

Rhonda's story makes me think of the story of Joseph in the Book of Genesis. Joseph, the favored son, wasn't so popular among his brothers. As a result, they sold him into slavery, and he was taken to Egypt. While in Egypt, Joseph found favor in the eyes of one of Pharaoh's officials, Potiphar. Then, after being falsely accused and imprisoned, Joseph found favor in the eyes of the warden and later with Pharaoh himself when Joseph was able to interpret his dream. Joseph went on to become a very respected and esteemed leader in Egypt—second only to Pharaoh—which came in handy for his brothers when a famine swept through Israel and forced them to travel to Egypt in search of food. Imagine their surprise when they discovered that the brother they had sold into slavery as a boy was now an official with great power in Egypt—power to give them food. Though the brothers didn't immediately recognize Joseph, he immediately recognized them.

When Joseph identified himself, the brothers were frightened that Joseph would seek retribution for what they had done. Instead, he forgave them. Joseph even moved his entire family, brothers and all, to Egypt where they were given the finest land and had every need met.

Yet as we read in Genesis 50:15, later Joseph's brothers worried that his attitude would change after the death of their father, Jacob. They sent a message to Joseph, proclaiming that their father's dying wish was for Joseph to forgive his brothers. Upon receiving this message, Joseph was saddened by their fear. He reassured them not to be afraid, affirming a powerful truth.

Look up Genesis 50:20 and fill in the blanks below:

"You intended to _____ me, but God

intended it for _____ to accomplish what

is now being done, the saving of many lives."

(NIV)

What Joseph's brothers did to harm Joseph, God used for good not only in Joseph's life but also in the lives of his entire family and their future descendants—God's chosen people, Israel.

Even when we are in the midst of horrible circumstances and pain, we can trust that God will redeem it somehow and use it for good. However, we have to be humble like Joseph, allowing God to shape and mold us through the process.

Rhonda's anger did not dissolve overnight. It took months for her to work through the conflicting emotions of grief until finally she was so tired of being miserable that she sought comfort from the God who had never left her. "I had been so self-righteous," Rhonda explained. "I had thought I was better than the man who killed my son because I had never driven drunk and never would. But God so lovingly pointed out that my sins were just as wrong—I was no different from him. It was as if my relationship with God had four corners and I had given Him three. I was still holding on to that last corner, and God wanted me to humble myself and surrender it to Him."

Rhonda had been raised in a Christian home and knew God's Word; but it wasn't until she immersed herself in His Word through the lens of forgiveness that the transformational healing began. She realized that if she refused to forgive the man who had killed her son, there would be two victims of this tragic accident instead of one. Thankfully, instead of believing what the world tells us about forgiveness, Rhonda chose to believe what God says about it.

That's when Rhonda decided to learn sign language. You see, the man who was responsible for her son's death was deaf and mute, and she wanted to visit him in prison and tell him that she had forgiven him.

Yes, you read that correctly. Let that sink in for a moment.

Rhonda spent months learning sign language while continuing to process her grief and raising three other children. When she finally met with the man, his family was present along with attorneys and police officers. She was modeling forgiveness not only to the man who had caused her such pain but also to everyone else in the room. God had transformed devastating loss and pain into a beautiful experience of mercy and grace.

That's the way God rolls, friend. He picks up the pieces of devastation in our lives and turns them into a beautiful masterpiece of redemption.

Read Isaiah 61:3 and complete the following statements about what the Lord gives to those who suffer loss:

A crown of _____ instead of _____.

The oil of _____ instead of _____.

A garment of _____ instead of a spirit of _____.

(NIV)

What does it say they will be called?

The verses that follow go on to explain how God will rebuild, restore, and renew whenever there is suffering. If you are walking through a tough time, sweet sister, I would suggest you read Isaiah 61 every day, allowing the hope and truth of these verses to penetrate your grieving heart!

Like Joseph, Rhonda allowed God to pick up the broken pieces of destruction in her life and rebuild them into a beautiful ministry. She will always miss her son and would give anything to have him back, but she finds redemption in the pain by ministering to countless families who have lost children due to drunk drivers. She gained wisdom and compassion that can be acquired only through suffering. Best of all, her relationship with God is more intimate than she ever could have imagined.

To the world, Rhonda's ability to forgive the man responsible for her son's death is unimaginable. When we can't understand how someone could forgive another person, that's radical forgiveness—the kind of forgiveness made possible only through Jesus; the kind of forgiveness He demonstrated.

Read Luke 23:34. How did Jesus show radical forgiveness, and to whom?

Can you believe Jesus asked God to forgive the very men who were torturing him as He hung on the cross? It's unimaginable. Radical. And that is exactly the same forgiveness He has for each of us.

When we're hurt by others, our emotions can take over, causing us to think the way the world thinks rather than the way God thinks. According to the world's standards, we should cast out of our lives those who have

One way others can see Jesus through us is by our ability to forgive—in all circumstances.

hurt us, seek revenge, make their lives miserable, and withhold forgiveness until they ask to be forgiven. While there are situations when we might need to establish some relational boundaries (we'll talk about that next week), because of Jesus it is possible to talk through a conflict, forgive, and have a closer relationship. In fact, one way others can see Jesus through us is by our ability to forgive—in all circumstances.

In First Thessalonians, Paul wrote to the believers of Thessalonica about imitating Jesus.

Read 1 Thessalonians 1:2-10 below:

2-5Every time we think of you, we thank God for you. Day and night you're in our prayers as we call to mind your work of faith, your labor of love, and your patience of hope in following our Master, Jesus Christ, before God our Father. It is clear to us, friends, that God not only loves you very much but also has put his hand on you for something special. When the Message we preached came to you, it wasn't just words. Something happened in you. The Holy Spirit put steel in your convictions.

5-6You paid careful attention to the way we lived among you, and determined to live that way yourselves. In imitating us, you imitated the Master. Although great trouble accompanied the Word, you were able to take great joy from the Holy Spirit!—taking the trouble with the joy, the joy with the trouble.

7-10Do you know that all over the provinces of both Macedonia and Achaia believers look up to you? The word has gotten around. Your lives are echoing the Master's Word, not only in the provinces but all over the place. The news of your faith in God is out. We don't even have to say anything anymore—you're the message! People come up and tell us how you received us with open arms, how you deserted the dead idols of your old life so you could embrace and serve God, the true God. They marvel at how expectantly you await the arrival of his Son, whom he raised from the dead—Jesus, who rescued us from certain doom.

(The Message)

Fun Fact

Thessalonica was located in the Roman province of Macedonia. Its harbor and proximity to a heavily traveled roadway helped believers to spread the gospel quickly.

In your own words, how would you summarize what Paul was saying?

There is so much depth here, but you know what stands out to me most? The part where Paul says, "When the Message we preached came to you, it wasn't just words. Something happened in you. The Holy Spirit put steel in your convictions." In other words, the Thessalonians *listened* and *heard* the Scriptures.

There's a big difference between listening and hearing, right? I can hear you talking, but I may not be listening. When we listen, we engage and care about what the speaker is saying to us. Clearly, listening to the Scriptures and taking them to heart through the Holy Spirit transformed the Thessalonians. As a result, their actions came into alignment with the words they had heard about Jesus and were, in turn, sharing with others.

A friend of mine who ministers to the homeless was talking to a group of people living under a bridge in a large city when one man stepped forward and challenged, "Show me what you say." If we want to model forgiveness to an unforgiving world, we have to show the people of the world what we say. We can tell others the importance of forgiving. We can read the Scriptures and believe God's clear words about forgiveness and acknowledge Jesus' example. But if we don't forgive, we aren't imitators of Jesus or the Word; and that creates a disconnect in our lives.

My friend Melinda is one of my dearest Heart Sisters because we have journeyed through two conflicts together with humility and forgiveness. It might be easier to flee a friendship when a disagreement surfaces, but as I've said previously, a true Heart Sister sticks it out and talks it out. A true Heart Sister imitates Jesus.

In one of my favorite books about forgiveness, *The Devil in Pew Number Seven*, author Rebecca Nichols Alonzo writes these wise words:

> Make no mistake about it. People are observing you and me to see how we, as Christians, deal with the hard knocks of life. When they see that we've been wronged, offended, wounded, ripped off, shortchanged, or "done a wrong turn," our response can either attract those who are watching us to the Savior or give them yet another excuse not to follow Him.[4]

People are watching. Let's attract them to the Savior by modeling forgiveness

Turning to God

Think about your actions during the past month. Have you attracted people to the Savior by imitating His forgiveness? If not, take heart. Each day we're given new mercies, and today is no different! Confess your struggle with forgiveness to God, and ask Him to give you the self-control you need for Scripture to transform your heart so your actions may follow. Once we choose to follow Jesus, the process of sanctification begins, which is the lifelong process of learning to be more like Jesus. So confess, repent, and forgive—beginning with yourself.

DAY 4: FORGIVING OURSELVES

Years ago, a friend of mine asked me to her home for dinner. I was about to run my first-ever half-marathon, and she offered to prepare a tasty pasta dinner and a night of rest and good conversation. At the last minute I canceled because that particular night was the only night that my boyfriend, who later became my husband, could help me to create the playlist I would listen to while running. I chose him over her.

When I called my friend to tell her, she was hurt—and rightfully so. She had not only purchased the food but also my favorite yellow flowers. My friend had gone to great lengths to offer encouragement and support as I prepared to do something out of my comfort zone—so far out, in fact, that I wasn't thinking straight. While I certainly am not making excuses, I confess to being immature and self-centered in those days. I've made some good progress, but I have no shame in admitting I still have a long way to go!

A few years later, I was married and had a young daughter. One night when I was cleaning up the remnants of dinner and rinsing dirty dishes, this situation came to mind. Suddenly I felt crippling guilt. How could I have been such a terrible friend? Then the downward spiral started. I'm guessing you're no stranger to that spiral. We gobble up the bait of guilt and wash it down with shame; and before we know it, we're ready to beg the wardens to put us in jail.

Yet what we often forget is that God, the ultimate judge, doesn't convict us. Through Christ, we are a forgiven people. What matters most is what we do after we sin.

I had already asked my friend for forgiveness, but I had failed to forgive myself. When God tells us to forgive others, He's including us in that group, too. Why is it sometimes easier to forgive others than ourselves? Why are we so hard on ourselves? After all, we are daughters of God, too.

After much prayer and surrendering the situation to God, I realized a painful truth: not forgiving myself is a form a pride. In order to understand that, let's first look at some Scriptures about God's forgiveness.

Look up the following Scriptures and summarize them in your own words below.

Scripture	Summary
Psalm 51:7	
Psalm 103:8-12	
Isaiah 1:18	
1 John 1:9	

What do these Scriptures reveal?

Sister, you are forgiven as far as the east is from the west. You're washed as white as snow and now are pure. If you've confessed and repented, you've been released from guilt.

You may have a horrible moment, but that does not make you a horrible friend.

In the situation I described, I had allowed the sneaky lies of shame to creep in and make me feel that I was a horrible friend, but that's just not true. I had a horrible moment, but I'm not a horrible friend. Apply that to yourself, my sweet sister. You may have a horrible moment, but that does not make you a horrible friend.

Shame is a dark shadow that creeps over our being and tries to paralyze us with lies—lies telling us that we're horrible; that our sin, rather than our Savior, defines us; that we will never be forgiven for the terrible thing we did. Perhaps you've been told hurtful things such as, "You ought to be ashamed of yourself!" or "Shame on you!" These are called word curses, and they can be difficult to release. Before you know it, you believe them to be true; it's called the self-fulfilling prophecy. When others repeatedly tell us something about ourselves, we start to believe it—even though it's usually not true.

Shame is so destructive that I wouldn't wish it on anyone, even my biggest enemy. God doesn't want us to live under the dark umbrella of shame, because it does not align with the truth. Remember how I told you earlier that I realized not forgiving myself was a form of pride? You see, it became clear to me that if God tells me in His Word that He has forgiven me and washed me as clean as snow but I do not believe Him, then I am choosing my own way by believing lies instead of His truth; and that is prideful.

I have made a lot of bad decisions and have done some terrible things in my life. But when I allow shame to take over, I forget a very important truth.

Read 2 Corinthians 5:17 and fill in the blanks below. (Your translation may be different.)

Therefore, if anyone is in _____, *the*

_____ _____ *has come:*

The _____ *has gone, the* _____ *is here!*

(NIV)

If you're like me, you know this truth but sometimes may need to be reminded of what you already know.

If you've done something in your past that you aren't so proud of, join the club! The thing about our journey through life is that we all mess up. I don't know anyone who hasn't done something she regrets or made a mistake he wishes he could take back or struggled with feelings of shame over a less-than-flattering moment. I could check every one of those boxes, sister.

We are new creations in Christ Jesus. Let that sink in a moment. You—yes, *you*—are a new creation.

But what if you've already become a new creation and then mess up big time? Well, again, join the club! Each day, you receive a special gift.

Read Lamentations 3:22-23 in the margin.

What never fails?

When do we receive them?

²² Because of the LORD's great love we are not consumed,
    for his compassions never fail.
²³ They are new every morning;
    great is your faithfulness.
        (Lamentations 3:22-23 NIV)

Some translations of this verse use the word *mercies* in place of *compassions*. That's right, friend. Every single day is a new day with new mercies and compassions.

I'm not saying we don't need to take responsibility for our sins. We don't get to do whatever we want and then bask in the knowledge we'll be forgiven no matter what. That's taking advantage of truth, and it's not OK.

However, there's a difference between holy conviction and spiritual attack. Holy conviction is the stirring of the Holy Spirit within you that serves as an alarm when you have sinned. It's a gentle nudge and will never condemn, shame, or belittle you. Through the Holy Spirit, God disciplines, teaches, and loves—much like a parent with a child. But if you are constantly brought to a place of shame, fear, and embarrassment, that is *not* holy conviction. If the voice you are hearing is a condemning one, it isn't from God. Romans 8:1 says there is "no condemnation for those who are in Christ Jesus" (NIV).

Read Revelation 12:10.

What names is the ancient dragon given in verse 9?

What is he called in verse 10, and why?

These verses tell us that the evil one is the great deceiver and accuser, who loves to hurl condemning judgment upon those who love God. He is the father of lies (John 8:44), who takes a little bit of the truth (the holy conviction you feel) and twists it into a big fat lie. But when we allow God to name who we are, we are no longer defined by our sins. Jesus died for all of it, and when we seek forgiveness with a humble and authentic heart, He grants it freely. I once allowed my sins, not my Savior, to name my identity; but now I know that it is my Savior, not my sins, who defines who I am.

Here's another great thing: we need to confess and ask forgiveness for a specific offense only once. After seeking God's forgiveness on multiple occasions for something I had done, it occurred to me that I didn't trust Him to be who He says He is. My own lack of trust was clipping my wings of freedom.

God doesn't want us to carry around our junk, sisters. Last week we read Matthew 11:28-30, but allow me to refresh your memory:

"Come to me, all you who are weary and burdened, and I will give you rest. Take my yoke upon you and learn from me, for I am gentle and humble in heart, and you will find rest for your souls. For my yoke is easy and my burden is light." (NIV)

Forgive yourself, friend! You'll be amazed by the freedom you feel. I read an anonymous quote that resonated with me, and I hope it speaks to you, too: "Forgive yourself for not knowing what you didn't know before you learned it." This life is a journey, and we have so much to learn as we go. Along the way, we don't know what we don't know. At times we mess up and regret things we've said and done. Sometimes we forget whose and who we are.

Yet there is rest from those heavy burdens. All we have to do is put them down.

Turning to God

Is there anything you need to forgive yourself? What have you not released to the Lord? Confess and release it to Him—for good.

If the Lord doesn't reveal anything to you, meditate on this simple prayer and record your thoughts in the margin:

Dear God,

Enlighten what's dark in me,
Strengthen what's weak in me,

Mend what's broken in me,
Bind what's bruised in me,
Heal what's sick in me and lastly,
Revive whatever peace and love has died in me.

Amen.

(Unknown)

DAY 5: LEARNING HOW TO FORGIVE

My daughter was a mere seven years old when her heart was broken. A girl two years older who lived in our neighborhood told another girl that she no longer wanted to play with Sarah. "She still pretends, and I'm over that," she told her friend.

I understand that; really, I do. Even though my child was hurting, I know that girls develop different interests as they get older. However, my daughter's heart was broken; and if you're a mom, then you know how hard that is for a mama bear to witness.

I talked with Sarah about how it probably wasn't personal. I told her that God wanted us to forgive the girl, and we talked about how we should pray for her. She listened for a while and seemed to feel better, but then the tears began to well up in her eyes again.

"I understand that I need to forgive, but I just don't know how," she confessed.

Can you relate? I know I can! In that moment of truth, my heart softened because I so get that feeling.

As we've discussed this week, the world views forgiveness differently than the Bible does. Forgiveness is one of those ideas that sounds good on paper, but when it comes time to actually live it out, it becomes much more difficult to comprehend.

Read James 2:8-11.

What is the "royal law" James talks about?

What does James say about those who show favoritism?

What makes someone a lawbreaker?

Now, let's read and unpack the next two verses, which are powerful.

Read James 2:12-13 and fill in the blanks. (Your translation may be slightly different.)

Speak and act as those who are going to be _____

by the law that gives _____, *because*

_____ *without* _____ *will*

be shown to anyone who has not been _____. *Mercy*

_____ *over*_____.

(NIV)

Following the royal law leads to freedom. So often we think that rules and laws are confining, but in reality they lead us to the path of complete freedom. Is there anything better than that?

But if we do not love others by showing them mercy, then get this: we, too, will be judged without mercy. Oh, sweet sister of mine, I do not want to be judged without mercy. I need all the mercy I can get!

So, knowing that we are called to follow the "royal law" and that we need a lot of mercy, let's focus on how we can show that mercy to others. Then we'll be eligible to experience that sweet freedom James talks about. I'd like to suggest four things we can do to be more merciful.

1. Meditate on Scriptures about forgiveness.

There are many verses in the Bible about forgiveness. When in doubt, truth will figure it out! Let's start with my favorite forgiveness verse:

Write Colossians 3:13-14, our memory verse for the week, below:

This is a great verse to recite when you start to feel the dull, nagging pain of unforgiveness working its way through your heart.

2. Pray for the person you need to forgive.

I know this is really, really hard, friend. I understand this completely and have even lived through it. When we've been hurt by someone, our flesh automatically reacts in defense. In full disclosure, I'm not always thinking nice thoughts of rainbows and sunshine when it comes to people who've hurt me—or those who hurt my children (remember my mama bear problem?).

Yet, we're supposed to pray for those who hurt us.

Read Matthew 5:44 and fill in the blanks. (Your translation may be different.)

"Love your _____ and pray for those who _____ you."

(NIV)

Something interesting happens when you pray for your enemy: your heart softens toward that person, and forgiveness becomes a little easier to stomach.

I disagree with those who say we must wait to apologize until we feel like we're ready. Sometimes action has to precede emotion. Likewise, we can forgive without the other person ever saying "I'm sorry." As I mentioned earlier in the week, I haven't always believed this. There was a time when I would not even consider forgiving someone unless he or she apologized first. But nowhere in Scripture does it say the offender must ask to be forgiven. Remember: forgiveness isn't for them; it's for you.

3. Understand that forgiveness is mandatory.

On Day 1 of this week, we read in Matthew 6:14-15 that if we do not forgive others, then God will not forgive us. Sure, we can choose not to forgive those who hurt us, but it will be at a very high cost.

Read Proverbs 10:12.

What does hatred do?

> Something interesting happens when you pray for your enemy: your heart softens toward that person, and forgiveness becomes a little easier to stomach.

What does love do?

An unforgiving heart leads to hatred, and hatred leads to further strife and anger. Therefore, forgiveness is required, not merely desired.

4. Ask God to reveal what's at the root of your inability to forgive.

Why are you unable to forgive? Is it pride? Do you always want to be right? Are you playing a passive-aggressive game that you believe gives you the upper hand as long as you don't forgive?

Forgiveness is a process. Sometimes we will have to choose to forgive for the same offense again and again and again. If we were like Jesus, we would forgive just once and move on with our lives. But we're not Jesus; we are disabled by the flesh. Sometimes that flesh allows some of the old feelings of bitterness and resentment to sneak back in, and we have to make the choice to forgive again. As I mentioned on Day 1, forgiveness is not a "one and done" thing. Like any other process, there are stages in forgiveness.

1. Grieve the hurt. Depending on the severity of the offense, we can't be expected to forgive immediately. If someone puts her foot in her mouth and says something that hurts my feelings, I'll most likely forgive her right then and there. But if someone abuses someone I love, it's going to take me a little longer to arrive at the place of forgiveness.

Give yourself permission as well as adequate time to grieve the loss that results from the offense. That is a normal and critical part of the forgiveness process.

2. Make a choice. You either choose to forgive, or you don't. If you do, you will eventually, if not right away, experience the freedom of forgiveness. Remember that sometimes action must precede emotion. So even if you still feel a bit of anger or depression, making the choice to forgive often leads you to the path of complete and authentic forgiveness.

If you choose not to forgive, I can say with complete certainty you will experience ongoing anger, resentment, and bitterness. It's not worth it; God doesn't want you to be held hostage by unforgiveness.

3. Forgive. When someone has hurt me, regardless of the magnitude of the offense, I verbally state that I have forgiven him or her—even if only in the privacy of my own home. My offender doesn't have to seek my forgiveness because forgiveness is for me.

4. Experience freedom. When you choose to forgive, it is as if a weight is lifted from your shoulders. In fact, you might even find that your own journey with forgiveness will lead to the healing of other areas of your life as well. The breaking of chains is the best part of forgiveness! But be prepared for the possibility that the weight could return in some measure, which brings us to the next part of the process.

5. Forgive again. Depending on the severity of the offense, you might need to choose to forgive again. Just as God doesn't expect us to work on every single area of our brokenness at once, He knows there is only so much we can take at any one stage of the healing and forgiveness process. For example, a friend of mine was molested by her father as a child. Through her own forgiveness journey, she forgave her father for violating her. Later she forgave him for stealing her innocence. Later still she released herself from any sexual dysfunction that may have resulted from the abuse.

Sometimes forgiveness can be an ongoing and cyclical process in which we find greater and greater freedom over time. Be patient with yourself as you are walking this path. Remember the best part of following Jesus is grace, and give yourself some of it, too.

As we close today, read Matthew 5:9 in the margin. Who does Jesus say are blessed, and what will they be called?

Blessed are the peacemakers,
  for they will be called
  children of God.
    (Matthew 5:9 NIV)

Choosing to forgive is seeking peace. Seeking peace is not necessarily being meek and quiet—a doormat for all to walk upon. It's not about people pleasing or being a pushover. Instead, seeking peace means choosing relationship over strife.

Sometimes peace-seekers—those who pursue healthy relationships—might be considered "pot stirrers" by those who do not understand the freedom of living in peace. People who are still bound by the chains of unforgiveness often will criticize those who have broken free. But don't be discouraged. If you are feeling a nudge from God to speak the truth in love and offer or ask for forgiveness, I encourage you to press on and pursue peace. That makes you a peacemaker, which makes you a child of God.

Turning to God

Forgiveness is not a light topic, friends. I pray you have felt God's comfort as you've worked through this week's lessons. I also pray that you have been able to break free from any heaviness of unforgiveness that might be weighing you down, for that weight is what keeps us from living in complete freedom.

Do you need to choose to forgive someone today? Do you need to forgive yourself today? Take a moment to reflect, writing your thoughts below or in a journal if you like. End your time thanking God for His gentleness and new mercies that are yours each morning.

THE FORGIVENESS BUSINESS

We do not forgive for other people. We forgive for _____.

Shimei Curses David

⁵ As King David approached Bahurim, a man from the same clan as Saul's family came out from there. His name was Shimei son of Gera, and he cursed as he came out. ⁶ He pelted David and all the king's officials with stones, though all the troops and the special guard were on David's right and left. ⁷ As he cursed, Shimei said, "Get out, get out, you murderer, you scoundrel! ⁸ The LORD has repaid you for all the blood you shed in the household of Saul, in whose place you have reigned. The LORD has given the kingdom into the hands of your son Absalom. You have come to ruin because you are a murderer!"

⁹ Then Abishai son of Zeruiah said to the king, "Why should this dead dog curse my lord the king? Let me go over and cut off his head."

¹⁰ But the king said, "What does this have to do with you, you sons of Zeruiah? If he is cursing because the LORD said to him, 'Curse David,' who can ask, 'Why do you do this?'"

¹¹ David then said to Abishai and all his officials, "My son, my own flesh and blood, is trying to kill me. How much more, then, this Benjamite! Leave him alone; let him curse, for the LORD has told him to. ¹² It may be that the LORD will look upon my misery and restore to me his covenant blessing instead of his curse today."

¹³ So David and his men continued along the road while Shimei was going along the hillside opposite him, cursing as he went and throwing stones at him and showering him with dirt. ¹⁴ The king and all the people with him arrived at their destination exhausted. And there he refreshed himself.

(2 Samuel 16:5-14 NIV)

Everyone has _____. Not everyone is going to _____ you, and that is okay.

David's Mercy to Shimei

[18] They crossed at the ford to take the king's household over and to do whatever he wished.

When Shimei son of Gera crossed the Jordan, he fell prostrate before the king [19] and said to him, "May my lord not hold me guilty. Do not remember how your servant did wrong on the day my lord the king left Jerusalem. May the king put it out of his mind. [20] For I your servant know that I have sinned, but today I have come here as the first from the tribes of Joseph to come down and meet my lord the king."

[21] Then Abishai son of Zeruiah said, "Shouldn't Shimei be put to death for this? He cursed the LORD's anointed."

[22] David replied, "What does this have to do with you, you sons of Zeruiah? What right do you have to interfere? Should anyone be put to death in Israel today? Don't I know that today I am king over Israel?" [23] So the king said to Shimei, "You shall not die." And the king promised him on oath.

(2 Samuel 19:18-23 NIV)

Humility is essential to _____ _____.

If you don't forgive _____, you're sinning against one of God's children: you.

I do not understand what I do. For what I want to do I do not do, but what I hate I do.
(Romans 7:15 NIV)

VIDEO VIEWER GUIDE: WEEK 4

1. Meditate on _____ about _____.

2. _____ for those who have _____ you.

3. Understand that in the eyes of God, forgiveness is_____.

4. Ask God to _____ what's at the _____ of your inability to forgive.

Week 5

BLURRED LINES

ESTABLISHING HEALTHY BOUNDARIES

Memory Verse

Am I now trying to win the approval of human beings, or of God? Or am I trying to please people? If I were still trying to please people, I would not be a servant of Christ.

(Galatians 1:10 NIV)

Just Between Us

I once had a serious addiction that controlled how I made decisions, negatively impacted my relationships, and made me feel exhausted, frustrated, and overwhelmed. What was it? People pleasing. When people asked me to do something for them—whatever it might be—I usually said yes because I didn't want them to disapprove of me or decide they didn't like me anymore. And often I said yes at the expense of what was best for my family.

Then one day my husband lovingly said "no more." No more over-scheduling. No more fear of who likes us and who doesn't. Oddly enough, I breathed a huge sigh of relief! I didn't even realize how exhausted I had become from my addiction. Our decision to pull back did not mean that we did not help our friends and family now and then. It meant that we began to assess our schedules, and if we saw that we had too much going on, then we lovingly declined.

Instilling boundaries often can be challenging for us as Christians because we are told to always be loving and kind. While we should always be loving and kind, we also have to accept that sometimes the most loving thing we can do is place boundaries in relationships.

I once had a friend who dwelled on the negative. Nothing was ever right. Even when I tried to look for the silver lining, we always managed to get back to what was wrong. After I would spend time with her, I would feel a little down and negative myself. You know that saying "When Mama ain't happy, ain't nobody happy"? Well, it's true for friends as well. Spending time with that friend wore me out physically, mentally, and spiritually. And then this mama wasn't happy! It was time for some relational boundaries. That did not mean I never spent time with her again; I just became wiser about when and how often I saw her.

I believe the reason many of us are so tired is that we don't know how to properly implement boundaries. Perhaps we've believed the lie that we aren't even supposed to have boundaries. Some of us may feel that it's too much effort to instill boundaries in a relationship, so we just grin and bear it.

This week we'll focus on how and why God wants us first to please Him, not "them." We'll see that sometimes we need boundaries in place to do that, and we'll consider how to determine and establish appropriate boundaries. Whether you're a people pleaser or just find yourself overscheduled from time to time for whatever reason, learning to set healthy boundaries is essential to developing authentic, healthy relationships.

DAY 1: THE HAZARDS OF LIVING WITHOUT BOUNDARIES

There I stood, exhausted and sobbing in my kitchen. My husband had just told me he was stressed out. Admittedly, much of it was because of the commitments I had made—commitments that allowed me to "please" everyone except those I loved the most: my family. At the time, I was leading a women's ministry at my church and I was a yes-girl. Need a meal after surgery? Yes, I'll do it. Are you lonely and in need of a friend? Yes, I'm your girl. Need someone to watch your kids? Of course, I will! Super Natalie to the rescue!

But here's the thing: Super Natalie got tired. She snapped at her children and was less than kind to her husband. He began to think she was a grouch and a little bit like that clanging gong we read about in 1 Corinthians 13. Worse yet, Super Natalie's children became confused when they experienced her impatience yet witnessed a smile plastered on her face when it was time to serve others.

Teaching our children that we are to love each other and telling them how important they are to us while acting in ways that don't match those truths is very confusing to them. We give Jesus a bad name when we exhibit an "I've-got-it-all-together-and-life-is-perfect" facade to the public and then spit venom at our loved ones behind closed doors. Exhaustion can be very destructive in our faith walk, sisters.

Super Natalie needed boundaries because, in the name of ministry, the very people she loved the most were suffering—not to mention she, too, was stressed out beyond belief. Can I get an amen?

Can you identify with my alter ego Super Natalie in any way? If so, how has a lack of boundaries affected your life?

Back then I was a new believer as well as a new mom and wife. I had no idea what I was doing, but I knew I wanted to do it well. I desired to raise my children in a healthy Christian home because, to me, that was the ultimate success. What I didn't understand is that you don't have to perform to earn God's love and raise children up in the faith. In fact, the best way to teach others about Jesus is to love them right where they are—and love them well. I love Madeleine L'Engle's perspective on this: "We do not draw people to Christ by loudly discrediting what they believe, by telling them how wrong they are and how right we are, but by showing them a light that is so lovely that they want with all their hearts to know the source of it."[1] Amen, Madeleine. Amen.

Loving people well does not include snapping in anger in response to small things that don't make much difference in the overall scope of eternity. My lack of boundaries led to exhaustion, frustration, and irritation. I also failed to understand that no matter how hard I worked, there still would be some people who didn't like me or didn't think I had done enough.

Our memory verse this week is Galatians 1:10. Take a moment to write it below:

This is another verse I need to tattoo on my forehead! (It's getting crowded up there!) We don't live to please anyone but God, sister. This is the adage of the People Pleaser's Anonymous group I keep saying I need to begin. I could be a charter member for sure!

When we live to please other people instead of God, we will be worked over and run over. Sure, deep down we might know all the verses about our identity and who we are in God's eyes. Those verses have penetrated our heads. Yet if we are struggling to say no to people, then those verses have not penetrated our hearts. Scripture means nothing if we keep it in our heads but refuse to release it into our hearts.

What Scripture do you need to release from your head into your heart today? Record it below:

Scripture means nothing if we keep it in our heads but refuse to release it into our hearts.

Our culture tells us a lot of lies about boundaries, and I believed them for so long. I wonder if you have believed these lies, too?

- Boundaries are not kind. We should love everyone, no matter what.
- I do not love my neighbor as myself if I establish a boundary in a relationship.
- Christians shouldn't set boundaries because it's un-Christian to do so.
- If I establish a boundary in a toxic relationship, I'll be the "bad girl."
- I'll just keep dealing with _____; that will be easier than putting up a boundary.

Anyone with me? Perhaps you can think of others.

What other lies have you believed about boundaries?

Boundary is not a dirty word, friend, though there are some who would like you to believe that it is (more about that later). In fact, establishing relational boundaries is one of the most loving things you can do for you and your family. Boundaries allow you to love others well and handle sticky situations with the kind of grace that would make Mother Teresa proud.

In Week 2 we read Proverbs 4:23 (NIV). Allow me to refresh your memory: "Above all else, guard your heart, for everything you do flows from it." Sometimes we have to guard our hearts by not allowing others to take advantage of us or by choosing to keep our distance from those who repeatedly hurt us. We also guard our hearts by laying at the foot of the cross the desire to please everyone.

In what ways do you struggle with pleasing others?

Do you know what was at the root of my do-everything-for-everyone affliction? Pride. Pride is a subtle liar that derails, destroys, and destructs. I thought I could be everything to everyone—that I could do everything, be everything, and know everything. I had it all under control. It was going to be all right. Sounds like I thought I was equal to Jesus, doesn't it? Oh, sure, I never would have *said* I was equal to Jesus. Heavens, no! But my actions sure were proving I thought otherwise.

When we try to do everything for everyone, we don't give Jesus room to do what only Jesus can do: provide for us in time of need.

Read 2 Corinthians 9:7 and fill in the blanks below. (Your translation may be slightly different.)

Each of you should _____ what you have decided in

your _____ to give, not _____ or

under compulsion, for God loves a _____

_____.

(NIV)

Did you catch it? God loves a *cheerful* giver! Not an exhausted, stressed-out giver, but a cheerful giver!

If you are exhausted and overwhelmed, then it's possible you might be serving others for your own accolades rather than God's accolades. Even Jesus knew when it was time to step away and rest. He knew when He needed time with His father. He knew when He needed to eat. He knew when He needed to travel to another region.

Jesus set boundaries because although He was fully God, He also was completely human. Jesus never did anything without love. In fact, even when He exhibited righteous anger, love was at the core of His anger. I love how Jesus shows us that establishing boundaries is actually showing love, not disrespect.

If Jesus needed boundaries, then surely we do too!

Turning to God

What experience have you had in establishing boundaries in relationships? Is this difficult for you to do? Why or why not?

> When we try to do everything for everyone, we don't give Jesus room to do what only Jesus can do: provide for us in time of need.

You can't serve others well if your own well is dry.

Take a moment to thank God for sending His Son to us—a Son with human limitations who needed to eat, sleep, and spend time with God; a Son who experienced righteous anger when those who were supposed to know better were not respecting the Temple; a Son who quickly reminded others of their own sin when they were pointing out the sins of others; a Son who understood that physical, relational, and spiritual boundaries were necessary to give and serve others. Remember, you can't serve others well if your own well is dry.

DAY 2: THE BENEFITS OF BOUNDARIES

Several weeks ago, one of the boys who lives in our neighborhood opened the gate leading to our backyard and strode through, looking for a lost basketball. Now, mind you, I have no problem with this. My sons run in a sweet pack of boys in our neighborhood, and I adore each of them. But still it felt strange to look out the window and see him walking around back there.

Boundaries are like the fence around your backyard. It's kind of weird when people just open the gate and walk in without permission, isn't it? Boundaries allow us to establish a firm foundation so we can love most effectively. That firm foundation is Jesus—the rock on which we construct our lives. Without that foundation, we'll collapse!

Read Matthew 7:24-27. When the rains come, what happens to those who have built their home on rock? What happens to those who have built their home on sand?

Rock:

Sand:

Though I know the rock in this passage represents the Word of God, God's truth, I think we also can use this comparison in our relationships. Relationships that are built on sand are filled with strife and consistently drain emotional energy. But relationships that are built on rock have a solid foundation of mutual respect and understanding. A healthy relationship is one in which both parties respect, care for, and value each other. They are willing to humble themselves and admit when they're wrong, and they seek forgiveness and reconciliation when conflict arises.

Unfortunately, many people do not understand how to have healthy relationships. Maybe healthy relationships were not modeled well for them in their childhoods. Or maybe they've been hurt so badly that they want others to hurt as much as they do. When I meet people like this, I feel sad because I see someone who is bound by the chains of the past. Actually, I don't always see their brokenness at first. Sometimes I'm initially frustrated and irritated with difficult people who treat me poorly. However, when I ask God to help me see them through His eyes, then I'm able to see their brokenness. And guess what? I'm broken as well. I want others to see me the way God sees me, too!

Although we're all broken, there's one factor that separates those who experience healthy relationships from those who don't: those who have healthy relationships try not to allow their brokenness to adversely affect those they love—and when it does, they acknowledge it and make amends.

In life we all encounter those people that Graham Cooke calls "grace-growers."[2] Grace-growers are those who get under our skin—who stir up dissension and love in order to be difficult. These people make us reach deep inside and dip into our reserves of grace, growing our grace capacity. Now, aren't we grateful?

If you've been hurt by grace-growers in your life, forgive them—but also understand that forgiveness does not necessarily mean you will feel emotionally safe with those who have hurt you. Forgiveness does not mean you will be best friends with the grace-growers in your life. It means you have chosen to let go of how you've been hurt because you understand that forgiveness is for you and not them. As you practice forgiveness, boundaries allow you to remain in relationship to a certain extent while guarding your heart at the same time.

Learning to set boundaries takes practice. Like anything else, the more we establish relational boundaries, the easier it becomes to hold them in place. Let's consider six benefits of boundaries.

1. Boundaries define the line so that we know when it has been crossed.

Like a fence around a backyard, boundaries are the unspoken—or sometimes spoken—lines of conduct that most people with healthy social understanding will follow. For example, my friend Sarah has a strict "no texts, e-mails, or phone calls" rule between the hours of 4:00 p.m. and 9:00 p.m. This is her family time, and she will not allow it to be interrupted! Since those of us who would call, text, or e-mail her know this, we understand why she doesn't respond right away.

For Christians, boundaries also are the moral lines we choose to walk (which relates to the next benefit we will discuss). As followers of Christ, we are called to hold one another accountable to His teachings and example, speaking the truth in love when others sin against us.

"If another believer sins against you, go privately and point out the offense. If the other person listens and confesses it, you have won that person back."

(Matthew 18:15)

Read Matthew 18:15 in the margin. What did Jesus say we are to do?

According to James 5:19-20, what happens to whoever "turns a sinner from the error of their way" (NIV)?

Boundaries help to hold us accountable—to ourselves, to others, and to God—which leads us to the second benefit.

2. Boundaries help us to maintain our roots in God.

When our identity is rooted in God's truth, we no longer allow the world to identify who we are. Instead, we are identified by who Jesus says we are, and because of our love for the Lord, we desire to live how He wants us to live. Anything that is outside the parameters of how God wants us to live can jeopardize our relationship with Him.

A friend told me about a situation that threatened to negatively impact her entire family and her relationship with God. One of her friends was having an extramarital affair, so when my friend's own marriage hit a rough spot, that friend encouraged her to find someone else and move on. Clearly that is not how God wants us to handle marital challenges! However, in her heightened emotional state, my friend started to wonder if that might be a good idea. Thankfully, because she had established moral boundaries, she did not act on her friend's bad advice and was able to maintain her roots in God. But we can see how someone without strong roots in the Lord, or boundaries to maintain those roots, might easily be shaken by bad advice during a difficult time.

Sometimes boundaries allow us to turn someone else away from sin, and sometimes boundaries help us to turn ourselves away from sin. In either case, boundaries that are grounded in God's Word help us to maintain a right relationship with God.

3. Boundaries communicate healthy expectations in relationships.

Sometimes our boundaries need to be communicated to others—such as when a friend repeatedly stops by unannounced during dinnertime, crosses the line when disagreeing about politics, or offers unsolicited advice in a critical and hurtful way. If personal boundaries are repeatedly crossed, we probably need to talk to the one who is doing the crossing. Lovingly telling people what to expect can lead to a relationship built on mutual respect.

Healthy expectations give us the freedom to be released from the guilt that might rear its ugly head when it's time to implement a boundary in a relationship. If you've communicated what you will and will not tolerate, then responsibility transfers to the offender if those boundaries are crossed. Truthfully, when others do not respect our boundaries, it is their problem, not ours.

4. Boundaries help us not to be overscheduled.

When we are busy, we don't have time to focus on what really matters. As was the case with Super Natalie, we can forget our family is our first ministry. When we base our identity on the approval of others, we miss out on living with the joyous approval of God. We believe the lie that our performance will earn our salvation, give us a higher social standing, or qualify us as Christian of the Year. When we equate a busy schedule with success, we often don't understand why we're more stressed! Busy schedules lead to burnout, and burnout means it's time to take care of you. We'll talk more about this on Day 4!

5. Boundaries help us to take care of ourselves.

Rest is crucial, and this doesn't just mean getting enough sleep. It also means not overcommitting and running from point A to point B like a chicken without a head! Self-care includes eating the right foods, exercising, and spending time with those who encourage you and love you for who you are.

Read Matthew 14:13-21. While you might be familiar with this story, try to read it with fresh eyes. Knowing that Jesus was fully God and fully man, how do you think He might have felt during this time?

Now, read Matthew 14:22-23. What did Jesus do after He dismissed the crowds? Why do you think He did this?

> **When we don't take care of our own physical and emotional needs, we can't give from our overflow because there simply isn't any overflow to give.**

During His time on earth, Jesus understood His needs as a human being. He knew He needed to pull away from the crowds even when there was still work to be done so that He could rest, pray, and eat. When we don't take care of our own physical and emotional needs, we can't give from our overflow because there simply isn't any overflow to give.

6. Boundaries help us to discern appropriate behavior.

When we are rooted in God and understand His boundaries for us, we have a keener gauge of what is appropriate and what is not. For example, at our house we have a boundary around what television shows and video games our children can watch and play. My three children have learned what constitutes appropriate and inappropriate television shows and games, so it has become easy for them to discern when a show or game crosses that boundary. This is important to me and my husband because we want our children to make the decision to watch shows and play games that guard their hearts even when we are not present. Without this boundary, they leave their hearts exposed to material they may not yet be emotionally ready to see.

Think about what life on planet Earth would be like if there were no moral boundaries in God's Word or civil boundaries in our societies. The world would be a very difficult place to live in without boundaries!

Read John 17:13-19. What did Jesus ask in verse 15?

We are meant to live in this world, which is full of demands, stress, and sin. But with God's help and appropriate boundaries, including the guidelines found in God's Word, we can navigate this world more safely. Knowing what is appropriate and not appropriate helps to protect us from evil—and from ourselves. God always desires to protect His children, and boundaries do that very thing!

Turning to God

When it comes to relationships in my life, sometimes it seems that part of my house is built on rock while another part is built on sand. The part on sand has been constructed by me; the part on rock has been built by God. What about you? Do you feel like your relationships are built on rock or sand? Or are you like me and feel they are built on both?

A relationship that is built on sand will not last when conflict arises. But a relationship that is built on the solid foundation of mutual respect and healthy boundaries will endure. Take a moment to ask God what relationships in your life are built on sand and what relationships are built on rock, and list them below. (Or simply pray about it.)

Relationships Built on Rock   **Relationships Built on Sand**
(Mutual trust, healthy boundaries)   **(Strife, emotionally draining)**

DAY 3: BOUNDARIES ARE NOT UN-CHRISTIAN

The other day I was talking to my friend—I'll call her Annie—who is struggling with a difficult relationship. Annie's friend—I'll call her Joanne—had repeatedly hurt Annie, and it was clear Joanne's own insecurities and brokenness were negatively impacting the relationship. Truthfully, Annie had had enough.

The caveat? Annie is a strong woman of faith who loves Jesus.

"But what if God is calling me to minister to Joanne?" Annie wondered as we sipped our coffee.

It's true that sometimes God calls us to minister to difficult people. It's also true that sometimes the best way we can love them is to establish a boundary. There are times when the most loving thing you can do in a difficult relationship is put a boundary in place.

I shared that reminder with Annie—one I sometimes need myself—but ultimately it is between God and Annie. Whether God wants her to minister to Joanne or to love her by setting an appropriate boundary, He will reveal that to her.

The same is true for you. If God wants you to minister to a particular grace-grower in your life, He will reveal that through prayer and the reading of His Word. However, if your grace-grower has repeatedly disrespected you, been unkind to you, and made cutting remarks that tear you down, you must guard your heart, sister.

Sweet friend, can we vow to stop believing the lie that boundaries are not Christlike? Boundaries are very Christlike because, as we saw yesterday, even Jesus set boundaries.

For a long time I falsely believed that I had to minister to everyone and be in relationship with unhealthy people because I was so concerned about what people thought of me. I was worried they wouldn't like me or would think I was a phony if I didn't give everyone my everything—and for a people-pleasing girl, that's a big, scary threat!

In addition to my own expectations, it also seemed that others expected me to be Super Natalie because I was a Christian—a Christian in leadership at that—and nice girls in leadership don't say no. Even when I stepped down from my leadership positions in the church, I still experienced those expectations due to the public nature of my blog. When I didn't pursue a relationship to the extent that the other person wanted to be pursued, I was labeled a phony. When I made a mistake, there seemed to be much less grace, and I was even accused of being unbiblical. When I said no to invitations for anything good, it was a rare occasion when someone said, "Good for you for looking out for yourself!" Instead, I was often met with criticism, and that criticism often suggested that my boundaries were un-Christian.

Take a moment to write our memory verse, Galatians 1:10, below. I know you've done it before, sister, but let's do it again. It's a critical verse when it comes to boundaries!

During that season of my life when I felt I could please no one and I was letting everyone down, a friend of mine directed me to Psalm 62. If you are struggling with feeling that everyone is criticizing you, then Psalm 62 is for you! It was written by David when King Saul was hot on his trail, chasing him all over Israel because of jealousy. Yet David had done *nothing* to Saul.

Read Psalm 62 and answer the following questions.

According to David, what does God offer us?

What words does David use to describe God?

How do verses 3 and 4 describe our enemies?

According to verses 5 and 6, what happens when we identify the Lord as our rock and our fortress?

Now here's the best part! Reread Psalm 62:7, and fill in the blanks below. (Your translation may be different.)

My _____ and my _____ depend on God;

he is my mighty _____, my _____.

(NIV)

Did you catch that, friend? Your honor comes from Him, not them. If others judge and criticize you behind your back for setting boundaries, that's between God and them, not you and them. See the difference? If you are following and obeying God by setting boundaries, then you don't need to worry about what others are saying about you. You might be the subject, but you certainly aren't the verb; the action will come from God, and God doesn't like those who judge. Judging is God's job, and no one else can sit in that judge's seat. If others try to take that role from God, watch out.

Read James 4:11-12. What does it say about those who criticize and judge?

I love to look up Scripture in different Bible versions. This is how *The Message* expresses James 4:11-12:

> *Don't bad-mouth each other, friends. It's God's Word, his Message, his Royal Rule, that takes a beating in that kind of talk. You're supposed to be honoring the Message, not writing graffiti all over it. God is in charge of deciding human destiny. Who do you think you are to meddle in the destiny of others?*

Ouch. Anyone else? I share this with you because it not only convicted me of my own talk and judgments but also reminded me that those who criticize and judge me are held to the same standard and expectation. Your honor comes from Him, not *them*.

Boundaries are not only healthy; they also are holy. If you are keeping your eyes on the cross and are sure you are hearing God's direction to put a boundary in place, then you're being obedient to Him if you follow through. There's nothing un-Christian about that, sister. Far from it!

Contrary to what some might think, implementing boundaries in challenging relationships does not mean we are ungrateful for what the other person has done or is doing. Rather, we are prioritizing the protection of our hearts. The healthy guarding of our hearts shields us from continual hurt. Sometimes those who have hurt us will continue to try to hurt us by passive-aggressive criticism or disrespect. The old adage "Hurting people hurt people" is true.

I have a friend whose ex-husband repeatedly puts her down in front of their children. Even though she has spoken to him about this repeatedly, he continues to do so. While my friend is grateful for her ex-husband's role in their children's lives, she also speaks the truth when they ask her about the lies they've been told. She has decided to forgive him (even when it's hard), pray he will stop putting her down, and lovingly speak truth to her children. She has established holy boundaries to protect the truth.

On the flip side, it's important for us to support the boundaries of others, as well. When someone says she can't do something you want her to do, the best response is "I'm sorry you can't _____ , but good for you for honoring your boundaries!"

Giving others a guilt trip can make those who have chosen holy boundaries feel as though they're doing wrong instead of mirroring Jesus by understanding their own limitations. I've experienced this firsthand, and I'm guessing you have as well. Be forewarned: there are steamrollers out there who just want to get their own way. They might try to run you over, but the more practice you have with setting boundaries, the less likely they are to flatten you.

Don't be shocked if people react negatively to your newfound freedom obtained through forgiveness and boundaries. You know the saying "Misery loves company"? It's often true. When your light starts to shine brighter, it can illuminate the darkness in the souls of others—and facing the deep and ugly trenches in their own hearts can be terrifying. Many people live with this darkness because they don't know any other way of living, they don't realize they are being held captive by their own darkness, and it's easier than confronting whatever placed the darkness there in the first place.

Some people might be jealous because they want the freedom they see in you and don't realize they can have it as well. It's also possible they don't want you to start living differently because then you might encourage them to do so as well—and some people are just fine being miserable. It's true that we are all broken and need to have compassion for one another, but this doesn't mean we should compromise our own health so that someone else can feel OK about herself.

If we live to please God, *how* do we do that? Take a look at what the Bible says about pleasing God: 1 Chronicles 29:17; Psalm 51:16-17; Psalm 69:30-31; 147:10-11; Proverbs 12:22; 15:8; Romans 12:1; 1 Timothy 2:1-3; Hebrews 11:6; 13:16, 20-21.

We will talk more tomorrow about prioritizing self-care because it's such an important topic. But as we bring today's lesson to a close, let's do a quick review.

Where does your honor come from?

When someone speaks badly of you behind your back or passes judgment of you, it's between_____ and _____ , not _____ and _____ .

Good work, sister! Keep working on memorizing Galatians 1:10, reminding yourself that we live to please God, not people. And thank God for that!

Turning to God

Have you recently judged or criticized someone—especially for setting a boundary? If so, confess it to God right now and ask Him to make you more aware of your words and thoughts.

Second Corinthians 10:5 tells us to "take captive every thought to make it obedient to Christ" (NIV). A friend of mine wears a rubber band around her wrist and pulls it every time she thinks a critical or judgmental thought. Now that's discipline! I challenge you to join me in trying that over the next few days. You might be surprised how often you have to pull that rubber band!

DAY 4: LIVING AN INSIDE-OUT LIFE

Friend, the fact that I'm writing about self-care today demonstrates that God has a wonderful sense of humor. It's true that we write out of our broken places, and let me just tell you that prioritizing self-care is a very broken place for me!

Super Natalie still makes appearances now and then. In fact, as I type, we are about to sell our house and I'm ready to put on a cape and fly out the door! So much needs to be done. Details scream for my attention. Deadlines await. In the midst of all that, I still have a husband, three children, two dogs, and a cat waiting for meals. And what's the deal with laundry? It's just so needy. It constantly *needs* to be washed and dried. It constantly *needs* to be folded. It constantly *needs* to be put away. Whew! By the time we get all those steps done, it's time to start all over again.

Don't think for one minute I don't know how blessed I am. I do. Yet I think we can still feel overwhelmed by the management of our blessings, and there's no shame in being truthful about it; we just can't dwell there forever. Well-intended comments such as "It could always be worse" or "In a third-world country, that wouldn't be a worry" don't help matters either. Even though there might be some truth here, God still cares about what worries and burdens you, no matter what.

Remember the words of Matthew 11:29-30 that tell us to go to Jesus and He will give us rest. He will take our burdens and, in turn, give us His very light yoke to carry.

Sister, did you catch that? He will give us *rest*. Rest. Yes, rest.

Is rest a foreign concept to you? I know you sleep or you wouldn't be alive. But do you *rest*? The difference between sleeping and resting is that the latter is time for you. Boundaries protect our spiritual, emotional, and physical needs. Remember: you can't love others well if your own well is dry.

Take a moment and honestly assess the state of your well. Is it full? Half full? Has it been dry for a long time?

What do you need in order to fill your well?

What is holding you back?

My husband does a great job with this. There could be a million things left on the to-do list with only twenty-four hours to do them, and he will still call a cease-fire to retreat and refuel. He has shown me that the world will indeed go on if I hit pause and take a moment to fill my well. Sure, stuff I think needs to get done may not get done, but you know what? So often the stuff that I think needs to get done is not really a very big deal anyway. I admit that sometimes I'm the one making my life more difficult than it needs to be.

Let's take a moment to unpack one of my very favorite chapters of the Bible: John 15.

Please read John 15:1-4. According to Jesus, who is God?

Who is Jesus?

What does the gardener do to dead branches?

What does He do for the branches that bear fruit, and why does He do this?

What do we need to do to ensure we will continue to bear fruit?

That's right: we cannot bear fruit if we aren't connected to the vine. The vine offers nourishment from the *inside out* to the branches and leaves.

A few years ago we planted a small garden. My son, who was three years old at the time, proudly planted a row of tomatoes and a row of green peppers. As soon as he placed them in the holes he had dug and covered them with soil, he impatiently inquired, "Now where are the vegetables?"

Isn't that so like us? We want the fruit right away. We don't want to have to wait for it. But that's not how it works.

It is the nourishment that eventually produces the fruit, and the fruit is the sweetest and loveliest part of the plant. Yet sometimes I get impatient, not wanting to endure the pruning part. I want to fast-forward through the pain and get to the fruit. I wish it worked that way, sister, but it doesn't. As with a living branch, it takes *time* to bear fruit.

The vine that provides nourishment and life lives in *you*. We'll continue with John 15 in a moment, but first, let's look up a few Scriptures about the importance of caring for our bodies.

Look up each Scripture and either write the text or summarize the meaning in your own words.

Scripture	Text or Meaning
1 Corinthians 6:19	
2 Corinthians 6:16	
Romans 8:11	
2 Timothy 1:14	

We often hear the phrase "Your body is a temple," but do we fully grasp the meaning of this?

If you have accepted Jesus as your Savior, then the Holy Spirit comes to dwell *inside* of you. The Holy Spirit is part of the Holy Trinity, which means that Jesus is living in *you*. You house the Son of the Most High King.

Now, think of where you go to church or any church in general. If that church were falling apart, would you want to do something about it? Or would you run through the halls, throw trash everywhere, and spit on the floors?

Of course you wouldn't! But so often I do the equivalent of this to the temple that is *me*—the one that houses Jesus as the Holy Spirit.

It's true that God sent His Son to the world so that we could be reunited with Him. His main reason for sending Jesus was to redeem us all, offer us hope, and ensure that we will spend an eternity with God in heaven. Yet another reason God sent Jesus is so we could see a tangible model of how we are to live our lives.

If we look at the life of Jesus, we see a man who was forgiving. Gentle. Filled with humility. Kind. Only angered with righteous anger. Loving. Truthful.

While it might be difficult to imagine ever fully achieving a heart like Jesus', God sent Him so we could become more and more like Him while still here on this earth. Of course, complete sanctification won't happen until we are someday united with Him. Until then, becoming more like Jesus through the power of the Holy Spirit within us is what we are to do.

While Jesus possessed all of the attributes listed above, there's something else He modeled for us: setting boundaries.

Read Luke 5:15-16. What did Jesus do as the news of his ministry began to spread and more people wanted to see Him?

I believe Jesus listened to the gentle nudges from His Father. When He needed to fill His well so He could love others well, He did. I'm sure there were still people waiting to be healed or those who just wanted to catch a glimpse of the rumored Messiah. Yet He still broke away from the crowds when He felt that nudge. Jesus understood that He needed to take care of Himself so He could care for others.

In fact, the Gospel of Mark identifies seven times in which Jesus went on a spiritual retreat—either alone or with the disciples.

Read the following Scriptures from the Gospel of Mark (it won't take long, I promise!), and write a brief summary for each.

1. Mark 1:35

2. Mark 3:13

3. Mark 6:30-32

4. Mark 6:45-46

5. Mark 9:2-13

6. Mark 14:12-31

7. Mark 14:32-42

Scripture Challenge

Combining rest with God's Word is an excellent self-care practice! Here are some Scriptures to renew your mind, soul, and spirit as you rest. You might consider memorizing one or more of these verses: Psalms 23:3; 51:10; Isaiah 40:31; 41:10; Lamentations 5:21; Ezekiel 36:28; Matthew 11:29; John 7:37-38; Romans 12:2; 2 Corinthians 4:16; Ephesians 4:22-24; Philippians 4:6-7.

Jesus went to solitary places and prayed. He enjoyed intimate dinners with his closest friends. He needed rest. So, if Jesus the Messiah, the King of all kings, the Savior, needed these things, why do we think we don't? We are not exempt.

When we don't prioritize our own physical, spiritual, and emotional needs, we aren't taking care of the temple that houses the Holy Spirit. When we continually keep going, going, going without a break, thinking we'll be fine only to lose it while trying to make dinner, help with homework, or fold laundry, we aren't helping anyone. In fact, we are hurting everyone.

The world *will* go on if you stop to rest, friend. And you can say that right back to me!

Turning to God

Make one tangible goal for self-care this week and write it in the margin. It would be even better if you could establish two or three self-care goals in the next week, but we'll start small.

Take a moment to ask God to help you discern those gentle nudges telling you it's time to rest. In fact, if you're in a spot to do so now, go rest! Give thanks to the God who quiets your soul and gives you hope in a noisy world.

DAY 5: LIVING ON THE OFFENSE: THE WHEN AND HOW OF BOUNDARIES

Recently my husband confronted me with something I had been doing that bothered him. I wish I could tell you that I took his criticism well, but I would be lying if I did. Instead of listening to him, I started to formulate my defense like any good lawyer. Like any good war general, I began to strategize my attack. I refused to listen and instead thought of only one side: my own. I got defensive. I was more concerned about protecting my heart instead of hearing his.

Sadly enough, I've done this with some of my Heart Sisters as well. Sometimes I become defensive and formulate my response instead of really listening to what they have to say. I take the stance of protecting myself. Have you ever done that, friend?

When I think of protecting something, I think of walls. Sometimes these walls are a good thing, such as when we are protecting our children or another loved one. Yet often we build walls around ourselves because it's utterly terrifying to let someone through the gate. That's a lonely way to live, isn't it?

God created us with a longing to be fully known. We are fully known by God; there's not one thing about us He doesn't know. For crying out loud, He knows how many hairs we have on our heads (Luke 12:7)! It's also great to be truly known by a person we love. Though that person will never know us as well as God knows us, it's still very special to share that intimacy with another human being.

Defensiveness blocks intimacy. When we become defensive, we are putting our own needs above the person who is confronting us; in our struggle to be vulnerable, we lack the humility that is necessary in order to really listen. We build a wall that keeps us from the intimacy we were created to experience.

Of course, let's be real: sometimes people confront us with not-so-nice intentions. Perhaps they want to prove to the world that we aren't the Christians we say we are. Maybe they're so insecure it brings them great satisfaction to tear us down. It's possible they are hurting so intensely that they want someone else to hurt as well. Or maybe it's as simple as they love drama, and we're their next co-star. When we are confronted by someone like this, getting defensive will only blemish our Christian witness, demonstrate that he or she has the power to get under our skin, and confirm that we can be relied upon to participate in drama. However, if we don't give our grace-growers what they want, eventually they will get bored and look for another victim who's willing to play their game.

Fighting back will fan the flame, but grace is a mighty extinguisher.

Read John 9:1-12. What happened in these verses?

Now read John 9:13-39. How did the Pharisees react? Why do you think they reacted this way?

How did the blind man react to the Pharisees? To Jesus?

Do you know why the Pharisees were so threatened by Jesus? Because if Jesus was really who He said He was (and He was), then that would mean their power would fade and their legalistic, pious ways would be exposed. Deep down the Pharisees might have believed that Jesus was who He said He was, but they didn't *want* to believe it because it would be too great of a loss for them. They were in denial because of their own selfishness.

Now read John 9:40-41 and 10:1-18. How did Jesus respond to the Pharisees?

> **Fighting back will fan the flame, but grace is a mighty extinguisher.**

Jesus certainly didn't get defensive, because He understood that might make Him appear guilty. He listened to the Pharisees and then continued to peacefully teach about who He was and is.

How do you think you would have reacted if you were in Jesus' place?

When you are accused of something, how do you respond?

Read John 10:19-21. How did the Jews respond to Jesus?

When we don't get defensive when confronted but listen and then lovingly respond, we are following the teachings of Jesus. I don't know about you, but my natural response is not to respond as Jesus did—which is why self-control must come into play here. We have to choose to go against our flesh in situations like this, and it can be very difficult. Yet in the end, the reward of going against the flesh is always fruitful.

Though we are responsible for our own responses, it's also true that grace-growers sometimes exceed their growing season. How do we know when it's time to establish a boundary in a relationship?

A relationship might be crying out for boundaries if

- the offender repeatedly mistreats you and makes indirect, biting remarks that don't seem so bad but are intended to take you down a bit. This is called covert aggression.
- there is an obvious lack of humility when you attempt to talk to the other person about your own hurt.
- she repeatedly spins the issue so that you leave the conversation feeling you're always in the wrong—and never her.
- you notice that you're consistently beaten down rather than built up when you leave her company.
- she doesn't have your best interests at heart—only her own. She has an "all about me" mind-set.

The fact remains, sister, that sometimes we *allow* others to treat us the way they treat us. If someone repeatedly mistreats you, you have every right to implement some boundaries. In fact, it's encouraged because, remember, above all else you must guard your heart!

In 2 Samuel 6, we read that King David and his men had recently defeated the Philistines and were carrying the recaptured ark of the covenant back to Jerusalem. It was a huge honor to transport the ark, and it was an even bigger honor to house the ark in the holy city. Therefore, David was celebrating and rejoicing—along with many others.

However, David's wife, who was the daughter of Saul, didn't see it the same way.

Read 2 Samuel 6:16. How did Michal respond to David's celebratory spirit?

Now read 2 Samuel 6:20-23. How did Michal react when David returned to their home?

How did Michal greet her husband?

What was David's response?

Despite his wife's disapproval, David wasn't going to allow her to rain on his parade. By trying to shame him, Michal hoped to take away some of his joy. We don't really know why she was so angry about her husband's public celebration, but perhaps she still felt some loyalty toward her father, King Saul. Maybe she was angry that she wasn't a part of the processional that was carrying the ark. Maybe she didn't like David being away for so long. Who knows?

Here's the thing: it doesn't really matter why Michal reacted the way she did. Whatever the reason, that was *her* issue. However, David was free to choose how he would respond to his wife; and instead of giving her the power to control his emotions, he spoke the truth with love.

Rather than fall for her attempt to shame him, David understood that Michal's criticism was not from God; therefore, the matter was between God and her, and there was not much he could do about that. Likewise, we cannot control how others will treat us, but we can control *how* we will react—which includes setting boundaries.

I think it's important to address some common mistakes we can make with relational boundaries. As we consider these five mistakes, we'll also consider five important steps to setting relational boundaries.

1. Failing to have any boundaries at all. Life is in a constant state of chaos when no boundaries exist. Children go to bed when they want. Dinner is eaten whenever everyone is hungry, and then it's everyone fending for themselves. Calls are taken during family time, and people stop over unannounced. Friends and family dump their problems off at all hours of the day and expect you to be there. Not having boundaries leads to chaos, confusion, and most of all, exhaustion. A life without boundaries is a life with chaos, confusion, and craziness.

Step 1 in setting appropriate boundaries is to identify appropriate limits that will help to restore and preserve peace in your relationships and life.

2. Not communicating boundaries. I once found myself in a tough situation with a friend, and it became obvious that I would need to put some boundaries in place in our relationship. I felt I needed to retreat a bit so I could re-center and hear from God about this particular friendship. The problem was that I didn't communicate this to my friend. She felt abandoned and hurt that I had pulled away so abruptly, and in retrospect, I completely understand why. I should have communicated to her that I needed some space to sort through a few issues. Instead, I took the coward's way out and didn't address it at all because I knew it would be a tough conversation. When others know where our boundaries lie, then they can more easily respect them. However, if we play a guessing game with someone, then it becomes just that—a game. Emotional games are not only unhealthy, they're unkind.

Step 2 in setting appropriate boundaries is clearly communicating the boundaries to those involved.

3. Having inconsistent boundaries. Here today, gone tomorrow. This is a field of boundary land mines! When we integrate a boundary one day but don't follow it the next, we leave everyone, including ourselves, scratching their heads and wondering how to proceed. If we engage in gossip one day but refuse to do so the next, it's unclear where we stand with gossip. Eventually, resentment builds against the one establishing the inconsistent boundary, because no one knows what to expect.

Step 3 in setting appropriate boundaries is being consistent in upholding the boundaries we've set.

4. Being inflexible with boundaries. "Now, wait a minute, Natalie," you might be thinking. "Didn't you just say we shouldn't have inconsistent boundaries? And now you're saying we should be flexible. What gives?" I don't believe life is always black and white. It's true there are times when relational boundaries should be lifted for the sake of common courtesy. Several years ago a person who had repeatedly wronged a friend of mine said hello to her at a public venue. My friend returned his greeting. I was impressed with her grace and told her so. "I can't compromise courtesy and make the conflict worse by lack of maturity," my friend responded. "While I'm not going to engage him in conversation, I can respond when he has spoken to me because I'm not going to repay evil with evil." That is an example of amazing grace, indeed. Likewise, sometimes it is acceptable to be flexible with a boundary for the benefit of your family. For example, now and then on the weekend we will suspend bedtime for the kids and go to a late movie as a family. Though our kids get to bed later than usual, the memories we make and the bonding we experience are worth it.

Step 4 in setting appropriate boundaries is being flexible on occasion for the sake of common courtesy or unifying your family.

5. Having inappropriate boundaries. Please allow me to be bold and state something that isn't always popular to proclaim: I don't believe married men and women can be intimate friends with anyone of the opposite gender. Notice that I didn't say they shouldn't be friends. I said they shouldn't be *intimate* friends. There's a difference. Allow me to explain.

A friend I'll call Susan described her relationship with a male colleague as a "very close friend." She went to him for advice, sought him out for fun, and depended on him to cheer her when she was having a rough day. Susan eventually became emotionally dependent upon her male colleague, but she was married to someone else. She consistently sought from another man what only her husband should have given her, and they became emotionally connected.

When Susan's colleague retreated from their friendship, she was shattered. The more I talked with my friend about the relationship, the clearer it became: Susan's inappropriate boundaries led to a lot of pain further down the road.

Step 5 in setting appropriate boundaries is to honor and protect existing significant relationships through the implementation of boundaries. It's not a sin to proclaim that some relationships are more important than others!

Establishing boundaries can be like training for a marathon. The training period can be difficult. You'll have bad runs and good runs. You'll be tired at times and you might be inconsistent now and then. Thankfully, there is grace. I think most marathoners will tell you that the training can be grueling, yet there's not a better feeling than crossing the finish line. The same is true once you get the hang of setting appropriate boundaries: you won't believe the freedom you'll experience!

Turning to God

Spend some time asking God to reveal areas of your life that need boundaries. Do you need tighter boundaries with your time or in a particular relationship? Do you need help in viewing boundaries as healthy and holy? Do you need to stop trying to please everyone? Do you need to quit allowing people to treat you in a certain way? Feel free to write your responses below.

Thank God for giving us biblical examples to show us that boundaries are not only necessary but also healthy and holy. Praise Him for always looking out for you, protecting you, and providing for you.

BLURRED LINES

Am I now trying to win the approval of human beings, or of God? Or am I trying to please people? If I were still trying to please people, I would not be a servant of Christ.

(Galatians 1:10 NIV)

Loving our neighbors as ourselves does not mean regularly _____ them over our families or ourselves.

There are times when the most _____ thing we can do is establish a

_____ in a relationship.

1. When God shared the Ten Commandments with Moses

The Ten Commandments remind us that there are _____ to our sin.

2. When Jesus broke away from the crowds to tend to his physical and spiritual needs

We must take care of ourselves _____ and _____ if

we are to adequately love our neighbors as ourselves.

3. When Jesus comforted His disciples

Thomas said to him, "Lord, we don't know where you are going, so how can we know the way?"

Jesus answered, "I am the way and the truth and the life. No one comes to the Father except through me. If you really know me, you will know my Father as well. From now on, you do know him and have seen him."

(John 14:5-7 NIV)

If we want to be _____ with God and be fruitful, we must _____ in Jesus.

4. When Paul shared the truth about our salvation

Ephesians 2:8 tells us that God saved you by His _____ when you

_____.

First we believe by faith; then we are saved by God's grace.

Boundaries allow us to do something in order to achieve_____

_____.

Boundaries are not _____. It's un-Christian to allow those we love to

wallow in negativity, gossip, and _____.

Week 6

HEART SISTERS
DO'S AND DON'TS

PUTTING IT ALL INTO PRACTICE

Memory Verse

Take delight in the Lord, and he will give you the desires of your heart.
(Psalm 37:4 NIV)

Just Between Us

Soon after my book on friendship was published, I received a message from a lonely and heartbroken woman. She wrote: "I've tried to connect with women for years. I've gone to Bible studies, but I find myself always feeling left out. I've joined moms' groups, and it's more of the same. I've tried to be kind and giving and all those things you say to do, but I still don't have the Heart Sisters I desire."

After corresponding with this woman, she revealed a critical truth that is a factor in her loneliness: she doesn't know *how* to be in relationships with other women. She is not alone; I've since received messages from other women expressing the same frustration. I know how difficult it can be to develop authentic relationships. I've walked this path, too! So this week we're going to put it all together and consider some of the do's and don'ts of becoming Heart Sisters.

When we keep our friends on the pretty front porch but don't invite them into the messy living room, then we are likely to feel lonely. But if we are willing to get real and show our true selves to others, they will feel safe to do the same with us. Vulnerability is a necessity for developing authentic relationships.

When we always think our way is the right way, causing our friends to feel judged by us, then we are likely to feel alone. But if we are compassionate listeners and strive to understand different viewpoints, others will not feel judged. Feeling judged is a relationship killer, but mutual respect for differences leads to authentic relationships.

When we do not respect the boundaries of our friends—protecting their family time, marriages, or other priorities—then, you guessed it, we are likely to feel lonely. But when we respect those boundaries, we communicate that we're safe people who understand what is truly important and respect their priorities and needs.

These do's and don'ts we will explore are not always a magical solution. Like the first sweet woman who contacted me, we can do everything right and still feel alone. We need to remember that cultivating friendships is a process that produces fruit in God's timing, not ours. Sometimes His timing is immediate, and sometimes it takes longer than we would like. But we can be encouraged by Psalm 37:4: "Take delight in the Lord, and he will give you the desires of your heart" (NIV).

While we're waiting for the relationships we desire, let us take delight in the Lord—an easy task when we remember that God loves and treasures us, forgives us, and will never reject us. And let us be confident that He *will* give us the desires of our hearts!

DAY 1: HEART SISTERS DON'TS, PART 1

I love a good inspirational quote, don't you? I have an ongoing collection of some of my favorites, but the one that resonates with me the most was uttered by none other than Mark Twain himself. "A man who carries a cat by the tail can learn something he can learn no other way," he wisely stated.

Oh, sister, let me just tell you—I have carried the cat by the tail so often I'm certain I have permanent scars on my forearms from scratches and bites. Have I mentioned that I can be a slow learner?

We're going to spend the next two days talking about what a Heart Sister doesn't do, but there is something I need you to know. We've all, every single one of us, done some of the things we are going to be discussing, and I want you to remember something: there is no condemnation in Christ Jesus. Never, ever, ever. In fact, I want us to start this day by looking at that very passage.

Read Romans 8:1-2 and either write the verse below or paraphrase its meaning:

This may be a verse you're familiar with, but I wanted you to read it again; it's that important.

I also want you to recall Lamentations 3:22-23, which we discussed on Week 4, Day 4. These verses remind us that because God loves us, His compassions never fail; He gives us new mercies every single morning. Each day is a blank slate. Does that give you hope like it does me, friend? It gives me great joy to know I start each day with a blank slate.

So with the understanding that there is no condemnation in Christ Jesus and that we are given a blank slate each day, let's talk about a few things Heart Sisters don't do.

A Heart Sister does not gossip.

Read Psalm 41:4-13. How does the psalm writer describe those who are gossiping in verse 5? What are they pretending to be in verse 6?

> **Gossip is a slippery slope, and it's difficult to regain traction when you've started to slide.**

This is a hard one for us, sister. Since we are relational beings, we like to know what's going on relationally with everyone else. Sometimes that curiosity gets the best of us, and our conversations go from "concern" and "prayer requests" to fulfilling our own curiosity and gossip.

Gossip is a slippery slope, and it's difficult to regain traction when you've started to slide.

So what's a girl to do when she finds herself in the midst of conversations that wouldn't be pleasing to God?

The answer to this question isn't "one size fits all." In fact, much will depend on your personality. I do believe that God asks us to be bold in our faith, but that can be terrifying for introverts. Wait—what am I saying? It can be terrifying for extroverts, too.

I also struggle with the concern that I might be sounding self-righteous. Truthfully, if we are doing what God wants us to do and honoring Him, then it shouldn't matter what people think of us. And yet, we're all human and struggle with this.

Read Proverbs 26:20-21 and complete the following analogy based on these verses.

A gossip is like _____ for a fire. It makes the

flame _____ bigger!

Now read Proverbs 26:22. What are rumors according to this verse?

This sounds a bit confusing, doesn't it? Aren't choice morsels a good thing? Well, yes, they are. However, this verse isn't meant to encourage gossip. It means that like good food, we will always be looking for more. Once we eat the nectar of gossip, we'll just want more and more.

The best thing to do when you feel like you're in a situation where gossip is spreading faster than a wildfire is to get the hose and put it out. If you can boldly speak up and say you're uncomfortable with the conversation, then do it. However, if you would like to be able to do this someday but need to work toward it, that's OK, too. Try to change the subject or if you must, get up and go to the bathroom. A little break from the situation will give you room to exhale and regain your footing.

Take a moment and read Proverbs 16:28. Write or paraphrase it below.

Do you want to be responsible for separating close friends? No, me neither. Let's not.

A Heart Sister is not honest.

That sounds crazy, doesn't it? Honesty is supposed to be a good thing, right? Author Tim Kimmel's book titled *Grace-Based Parenting* is one of my favorite parenting books. In it, he describes the difference between being honest and being candid.

When we are being honest, we are sharing for our own benefit. How many times have you heard someone flippantly proclaim, "Well, I'm just being honest!" or "Just keepin' it real"? Good for them—whatever they needed to release is now off their chest. These reasons do not give us permission to share something that would be injurious to another person. However, often what that honest person fails to do is think of the heart of the person who is receiving the "gift" of their honesty.

When we are candid, we speak difficult truths in complete love while protecting the dignity of the other person's heart. See the difference?

You can't fake this either. I confess I've veiled my candid conversations under the guise of protecting the listener's heart when really I was being honest. I made it more about me than her. Yuck. I hate to even type this, but I'm comfortable revealing some dark, ugly truths of my soul with you.

I know we have already read this verse, but I'm going to ask you to read it again because it's a truth we need to be reminded of often.

Please read 1 Samuel 16:7 and complete the blanks below. (Your translation may be different.)

*People look at the _____, but the L*ORD *looks*

at the _____.

(NIV)

God knows our hearts, friend. We can run, but we can't hide. This is a good thing, and a convicting thing as well, isn't it?

A Heart Sister does not stir up conflict.

Have you ever known someone who thrives on drama? For my southern sisters, let's just say, "Bless her heart." This desire for relational drama and conflict may temporarily fill a hole in her heart, but it is exhausting for those who are pulled into the story.

Read Proverbs 6:16-19. What are the first six things the Lord hates?

1.

2.

3.

4.

5.

6.

What is the seventh item listed?

7.

Those who stir up dissension are those who thrive on drama. They find conflict exciting and feel at a loss when one isn't brewing. Yet here's the thing: just because they brew the drama doesn't mean you have to drink it.

Scripture Challenge

The Bible calls us to be honest, but it also encourages kindness and gentleness. For more insights on why and how we are to speak the truth in love, check out the following Scriptures: Romans 15:14; 1 Corinthians 13:1; Galatians 6:1; Ephesians 4:15, 29; 1 John 3:18; 4:20.

Of course, we're talking about repeated conflict. It's natural and normal for a conflict to brew on occasion. However, if one person is continually stirring up dissension, it might be time for some relational boundaries.

We've covered some important ground today. We'll continue our discussion of Heart Sisters Don'ts tomorrow. Now, let's spend some time with God.

Turning to God

If you can, spend five uninterrupted minutes with God. Find a quiet place and ask God to reveal how He wants you to be a better friend. This is not a time of condemnation; it is a time of conviction in the very best sense of that word. If you need to confess any wrongdoing, then do so now. The next step is to repent and move forward. End by giving thanks for God's gentle nudges and healing grace and mercy.

DAY 2: HEART SISTERS DON'TS, PART 2

Recently, my sweet friend Maddie and I were sharing lattes at a comfy table in the back corner of our favorite coffee shop. Maddie's marriage was in turmoil; however, the tears brimming in her eyes were not because of the marital valley she was experiencing. Two days prior, she had shared what was happening in her marriage with another friend. After listening, her friend proceeded to completely bash Maddie's husband.

"She told me that she had always thought I was too good for him and I should just cut my losses and get out," Maddie said with tears rolling down her pretty cheeks.

"And, you know," she continued, "maybe she's right. I've tried and tried to fix myself and our marriage, but I can't force him to grow up and be a better husband and father. It might be better for our kids if we just divorce."

It didn't take long for my own eyes to brim with tears. I know all too well about the pain of marital hurt; however, my own tears were because of the discouragement Maddie received from her friend.

Sisters, marriage is difficult enough. We don't need our friends joining the bashing-husbands bandwagon.

Maddie's friend is not a follower of Jesus, which highlights the importance of seeking wise counsel from a Christian sister or mentor. If you want to gain a biblical perspective, you don't want to enlist an unbelieving friend to offer advice.

In her vulnerable state, Maddie started to believe what her friend was telling her. The thing is, it's OK for her friend to have that opinion. Maybe Maddie's husband *does* need to grow up. Regardless, if a friend is talking about a trying marriage, this would be a time to listen and refrain from bashing the man she loves. Heart Sisters need to encourage, not discourage, one another's marriages.

Of course, I need to add this disclaimer: I do not believe women should remain in abusive situations. If that is going on in a friend's life, then a Heart Sister will speak loving truth and help her friend get the assistance she needs.

> **Take a moment to read Ephesians 4:29; 1 Thessalonians 5:11; and Hebrews 10:24-25. In a nutshell, what should we do for one another?**

Have you ever been around someone who talks only about herself? Bless her heart, right? This brings us to the next item on our Heart Sisters Don'ts list.

A Heart Sister will not talk more than she listens.

Oh, sure—there are times when you need to talk and possibly might dominate the conversation when you're with a friend. However, when this happens repeatedly and your friend never gets the chance to talk about herself, you'll eventually exhaust her. After a while, she might start to resent spending time with you, thinking of excuses why she can't get together anymore.

> **Read James 1:19-21 and fill in the blanks below. (Your translation might be different.)**
>
> *Everyone should be _____ to listen, _____*
>
> *to speak and _____ to become angry.*
>
> *(NIV)*

Why should we do this?

What can we do to achieve this?

I don't know about you, but sometimes I find it difficult to be quick to listen. I catch myself being distracted when my children talk to me. I formulate my response while the speaker is talking instead of really listening. And I am guilty of sometimes thinking about what's next on my schedule when others are talking. I see the selfishness in this. Oh yes, I do! My late grandmother always said, "You have two ears and one mouth for good reason!" I think this is a good adage for all of us to remember.

A Heart Sister won't always turn the conversation back to herself.

Similar to not talking more than we listen, not turning the conversation back to yourself is more others-focused than self-focused.

Read Philippians 2:1-4. What does Paul say we should do?

> When I make my conversations all about me, it's only a matter of time before my friends flee.

When I make my conversations all about me, it's only a matter of time before my friends flee. And who can blame them? Good friends aren't preoccupied with their own content; they're content to hear the content of others first. Of course, there are exceptions such as when you have exciting news or are going through a rough time and need to process. I'm talking about a consistent pattern of behavior here!

A Heart Sister also will not play emotional games with you.

Among tweens and teens, this is called "emotional bullying." However, I've seen some emotional bullying going on in the realm of adults that would make the hair on the back of your neck stand up! Have you ever realized after two minutes into a conversation you've been sucker punched? While I once believed this was called passive-aggression, I recently learned it's actually considered covert-aggression.

The person who is covertly aggressive will often be seen as incredibly charming and warm on the outside but really has an agenda or anger festering on the inside. The covertly aggressive personality knows your own vulnerabilities and will exploit them to either feel better about herself or to get you to do something in her favor. She is very adept at cloaking her feelings and expectations, which is why it's so confusing when we find ourselves a victim of this kind of aggression.

Oftentimes, the covertly aggressive personality is unable to take responsibility for her behavior and is very good at spinning any concerns you might discuss with her, so that you leave the conversation feeling like you are the one who has done something wrong.

Emotional manipulation is alive and kicking in the culture of women. However, when we recognize it's happening, we are one step closer to making a positive change in the culture. So how do we handle a friend who is covertly aggressive? We recognize it is happening and we don't give her what she wants: the authority to name who we are or the power to manipulate us to do what she wants us to do.

Though it sounds simple, I know it's not, because I've been the victim of covert-aggressive personality types more often than I can count. The more you are exposed to this type of manipulation, the better you become at recognizing it when it occurs. Recognition is half the battle. When you refuse to be a pawn in the covert-aggressive's game, she eventually will move on and try to checkmate someone else.

A Heart Sister does not withhold forgiveness or lack humility.

I once had a conflict with a friend, and after it happened, she didn't want to talk about it. Instead, she preferred to sweep it under the rug and act like nothing happened. There was once a time when I would have gone along with that, but I can't go along with it anymore because I know it would impact our relationship. When I expressed this to her, she chose to end our friendship rather than talking through it. It was very hurtful.

When we choose relationship, God is pleased. When we choose strife, God is grieved.

Hear me on this, sister: you do not need to stand in the chasm of someone else's unforgiveness. Their inability to forgive doesn't have the power to hold you captive. Remember that forgiveness is not for them; it's for you.

However, it takes one to forgive but two to reconcile. You may never fully reconcile, but you still can choose to forgive with or without the other person's consent. But I have to say that if someone refuses to forgive or even attempt reconciliation, that equates to covert-aggression in my book. If you have experienced a conflict with someone who later seeks to reconcile, you have a choice in the matter. But if you refuse to at least attempt reconciliation, you are working against God's will. God is always for relationship—with Him and with others, particularly among His believers. Oftentimes what holds us back from seeking reconciliation is our own pride and fear—which is a lack of humility. Ouch. I know. I've been guilty of this many times.

We've come to the end of our Heart Sisters Don'ts list. Tomorrow we will be moving on to what a Heart Sister does do!

Turning to God

Pick one of the verses we have read today and insert yourself into it in the form of a prayer. For example, if you select James 1:19, your prayer might be something like this:

> *Lord Jesus, please give me the ability to be quick to listen, slow to speak, and slow to become angry. Help me to get rid of all filth and evil so that I can accept the word planted in me, which saves me! Amen.*

Be prepared to share your prayer with your group if you choose. Your courageous willingness to be vulnerable and share will inspire people in ways you may never know—serving a greater purpose.

Close by thanking God for His Word, which guides us in every aspect of authentic friendship.

DAY 3: HEART SISTERS DO'S, PART 1

"I just needed her, that's all," she said with tears streaming down her face. "She didn't have to do anything or say anything. I just wanted her to sit with me for a while."

My new friend described the pain of a missing friend—a friend she loved but who was nowhere to be found when she needed her the most. My friend was struggling with forgiveness.

"I feel like Job," she added.

Read Job 2:11-13. What did Job's friends do?

Job lost most of his family and earthly possessions. When his friends heard this, they offered comfort, support, and encouragement simply by showing up. They sat with him for seven days and nights and didn't say a word. Can you imagine? I have a hard time keeping my mouth shut when I go to comfort a friend. I'm in awe of their self-control.

Job's friends showed up and were present at a time when he felt beaten down and alone.

A Heart Sister will step in when everyone else wants to step out.

There have been times when I've been afraid to show up when I know someone is hurting because I was too worried about the "what ifs." What if I say something insensitive? What if their pain triggers something in me? What if it will require more time and energy than I can give? My guess is that at one time or another you've felt that way too.

A Heart Sister is willing to show up and step in.

We live in a busy and fast-paced culture of appointments, family activities, and other obligations that can dictate our time and energy if we allow it. Running at full speed keeps us from slowing down enough to walk with the hurting. We live a distracted and less compassionate life when we have so much going on that we fail to see the needs around us. When we're constantly plugged in, it becomes harder to unplug. But when we close the door on distractions, we open the door to hearing from God.

It's true that sometimes we can utter words that come off as insensitive, but it's what we do after we say those insensitive words that matters most. A heartfelt apology goes a long way. So does a simple "I don't know the right words to say, but I'm here for you."

In A. A. Milne's *The House at Pooh Corner*, Piglet and the beloved Winnie are best friends. I love this passage:

A Heart Sister
will step in when
everyone else
wants to step out.

Piglet sidled up to Pooh from behind.

"Pooh!" he whispered.

"Yes, Piglet?"

"Nothing," said Piglet, taking Pooh's paw. "I just wanted to be sure of you."[1]

We can be sure of our Heart Sisters.

A Heart Sister speaks the truth softly—even when it's hard.

After seven days, Job broke the silence by lamenting to his friends and wondering why such pain was happening in his life. Yet sadly, all three of his friends followed with thoughts that were less than encouraging.

Read Job 4:7-8. What did Job's friend Eliphaz suggest? (Hint: You might want to read other translations of these verses to gain clarity. *The Message* or the New Living Translation are good options.)

Eliphaz argued that the innocent do not suffer. He believed in the old school of thought that those who suffer must have done something wrong and therefore are being punished.

The other two friends, Bildad and Zophar, echoed Eliphaz's reasoning (see Job 11:1; 8:20). They took the biblical concept of "you reap what you sow" a little too literally and applied it a little too broadly.

Then in walked Elihu. Elihu waited until the other men were finished speaking because he was younger than Job's friends, and in that culture and time, you didn't speak until your elders were finished speaking.

Read Job 32:1-3. Why was Elihu angry?

At first Elihu seemed to agree that God was punishing Job for sin, and he was angry that Job would not admit his sin. He was also angry with Job's friends for not being able to answer Job's arguments. I should also point out that scholars often disagree on whether or not Elihu was a "good guy" or a "bad guy." I lean more toward the good guy team because later

Elihu points out that although Job was not without sin, his trials were not happening *because* of his sin. If all trials were punishment for sin, then we all would deserve Job's fate, wouldn't we? I'm thankful that the tough times we experience in life are not punishment but can be used by God to refine us. Job is an example of a righteous person who is refined through adversity, and I'm guessing you, like me, can relate.

Read Job 33:12. What promise did Elihu offer Job that Eliphaz, Bildad, and Zophar failed to mention?

It was Elihu, the youngest of this group of men, who offered the truth that God is greater than we are and anything we might face—wisdom and encouragement Job surely needed to keep going; words meant to shift Job's focus from himself to his great God. Heart Sisters speak truth softly—even when it's hard. They show up, stay in the game, and offer love to those who are hurting. Their presence is the present—a gift that will always be remembered by a hurting friend.

Read Proverbs 17:17 and write or summarize it below.

A Heart Sister stays by your side in times of adversity. I met my friend Jennifer in sixth grade, and though I don't get to see her nearly enough now, we've walked through many life stages together. She experienced the dreadful ups and downs of high school with me. She then walked through the painful end of my first marriage and a tumultuous period of dating that followed. I spoke at her mother's funeral; she was there when my father died. She shared my excitement when I met the real Mr. Right, and I asked her to be the only member of my wedding party when I married him. She sat next to me while I soaked my naked, hormonal body in the tub and cried that I should have never been trusted to bring a baby home from the hospital. In other words, Jennifer could teach a class on how to be present for a friend.

While it's true we need to stand by our friends, that doesn't mean that all boundaries are off. Sometimes people have made bad choices, and they want a coconspirator instead of a Heart Sister. Standing by a friend during times of trouble doesn't mean you need to participate in any bad choices or sin that may be taking place. It just means you are there to love her—without judgment and without compromising your own values.

A Heart Sister will work through conflict with humility and seek reconciliation.

You may have guessed that I was going to sneak in one more nugget about the virtues of humility. When we find ourselves in the mess of a conflict with a friend, how we walk through that conflict is crucial. If we refuse to see our friend's perspective, deny responsibility, become defensive, and start to point out her faults, then we aren't handling the conflict with humility and the friendship will very likely end. As we've discussed before, it's not necessarily the mistakes we make that ruin a relationship; it's what we do afterward that's most important.

If a friend comes to us and wants to talk through something hard, it's our responsibility as a Heart Sister to listen to her perspective without interrupting. We must apologize for hurting her in any way and take responsibility as appropriate; then she will know we are a safe and trustworthy Heart Sister. Humility communicates safety in the relationship, and safety leads to vulnerability. Vulnerability leads to authentic Heart Sisters. And authentic Heart Sisters are what we all desire.

Read Ephesians 4:2 and either write or summarize it below.

It's so important that we bear with one another in love because none of us is complete. We'll be complete someday, but not on this side of heaven. Therefore, we're all under construction and need others to bear with us, which means we need to bear with them, too!

Turning to God

Spend some time prayerfully reflecting on the following questions:

- Was there a part of Job's story that caught your attention? If so, why?

- If not, have you ever felt abandoned by friends? Discouraged by friends? Maybe led astray by well-meaning but unbelieving friends?
- Have you ever been a friend who has offered well-meaning but inaccurate truth?
- Have you ever been the friend who has abandoned another friend?
- Have you ever been the discourager?

Now, release and forgive those who have hurt you and those you may have hurt. Grace for all, friend, including yourself.

DAY 4: HEART SISTERS DO'S, PART 2

Several years ago, I found myself exhausted, frustrated, and burned out while serving in ministry. I had three young children and a husband who worked long hours. Laundry still needed to be done, meals needed to be cooked, and groceries needed to be bought and put away. All of this in combination with leading a women's ministry group led me to the point of crisis—specifically, in my marriage.

Marriage is hard work. Personally, I think if anyone claims it isn't, she or he is lying. Add other stressors on top of having young children, and you have a recipe for disaster. Super Natalie had said yes to too much. I was overcommitted and overwhelmed—and in desperate need of an overhaul.

Two of my Heart Sisters sat on a couch in my living room one rainy afternoon. Our children played while they spoke truth softly to my hurting heart. It was time to pull out of everything and focus on my marriage and my children. Katrina and Melinda helped devise a plan for alleviating my responsibility in the ministry and even threatened to take my calendar and control what I committed to do for a while. Now *that's* an intervention!

A Heart Sister points us to truth and encourages us to endure.

As I've said before, Heart Sisters speak truth even when it's hard. They also encourage us to endure in light of that truth. According to Merriam-Webster's *New Collegiate Dictionary*, the definition of *authentic* is "real or genuine; not copied or false."[2] I don't care what word we use to describe it;

at the end of the day, I want real and genuine friends who are not copied or false. Don't you?

There are times when I can fall into a pit and begin to hear voices that are not from God. *I'm never enough for anyone. I'm not a very good writer. I should be ashamed for yelling at my children like that.* My guess is you are no stranger to thoughts like these, either. I've had moments when I've found myself so far removed from truth that I've literally needed a Heart Sister to point out how off base I really am. I can always count on my friend Jill to say, "That's just not right or true." And she's usually correct: my thinking isn't right or true. This is when having believing friends who possess an understanding of how God operates comes in handy.

For example, when marital difficulties arise, the world often encourages an individual to take a stand against how she or he is being treated and leave the spouse. On the other hand, a friend who is a believer would likely encourage a person to hang in a bit longer before making a rash decision that will have big impact. She understands marriage can sometimes be hard, but if we flee when it gets tough, we miss out on a deeper relationship with our husband—and with God. Heart Sisters who point us back to truth can encourage us to endure those times when life is just plain hard.

A Heart Sister is loyal and mirrors the love of God.

While truthfulness is extremely valuable in our friendships, loyalty is as well. Heart Sisters are steadfast in their love for us and will never leave us behind. They're loyal and unwavering.

Read 2 Kings 2:1-17. Who is involved in these passages?

Elijah was a prophet who spoke painful truth to those who didn't always want to hear it. He knew that his time on earth was coming to an end; therefore, God led him to Elisha to be his successor. Elijah served as a mentor to Elisha, and Elisha deeply loved Elijah.

What did Elisha tell Elijah three different times?

When I read these verses, I am reminded of some of the promises God has made to us. Holy Heart Sisters mirror the love God has for us.

Read the following Scriptures and write or summarize each.

Deuteronomy 31:6	
Joshua 1:5	
Joshua 1:9	
Matthew 28:20	
Hebrews 13:5-6	

What is the main message these passages communicate to us?

Like God, a holy Heart Sister will stand by us, no matter what. However, there is one disclaimer: a Heart Sister will stick by us no matter what *as long as she is not repeatedly being treated unkindly or disrespected*. As we learned last week, boundaries are not only healthy; they also can be holy. However, when both parties are healthy, Heart Sisters will be there for each other *always*—much like God is there for us always.

How can you know when you have a loyal Heart Sister? If you know your friend would defend you if someone else was speaking not-so-kindly of you, then you've got a loyal friend you can trust to have your back. A Heart Sister cares for you and looks out for you. Your well-being is of the utmost importance to her because she knows her well-being is of the utmost importance to you. When Heart Sisters have each other's backs, then they can safely be assured their friendship is authentic and rock-solid.

> **Read 1 Samuel 18:1-4. What do we learn about the relationship between David and Jonathan? What did Jonathan do to show David his devotion?**

You know what I love the most about the friendship of Jonathan and David? Even after Jonathan's father, King Saul, turned his back on David and tried to kill him, their friendship remained intact. In fact, Jonathan remained loyal to David until Jonathan died; and as we read in Week 4, David honored Jonathan's son, Mephibosheth, with a place at his table and a place to live for the rest of his days.

A Heart Sister encourages us to be the best we can be.

When we are believing lies and our Heart Sisters speak the truth we need to hear and stand by us no matter what, they're also encouraging us to grow spiritually and mentally. To put it simply, Heart Sisters encourage us to be the best we can possibly be.

> **During Week 1, we looked up Proverbs 27:17. Take a moment to refresh your memory. What wisdom is shared in this verse?**

There's a popular saying, "Show me your friends and I'll show you your future." It's a fact that we tend to behave like the people who surround us. Yes, you can be a light for others, but it's far easier for your light to dim when you're the only one shining!

If you look at the life of Jesus, He spent time with both sinners and those who were faithful. I think this is a good model for us to follow as well. If we don't ever spend time with those who don't believe, then we aren't really doing what Jesus has commanded us to do—make disciples of all nations and love our neighbors as ourselves. On the other hand, if we never spend time with other believers, we have less encouragement and accountability to stay on that narrow path—and we lack the wisdom we can glean from the biblical perspective of Christian friends.

Read Proverbs 19:20 and write or summarize it below:

Discipline and instruction do not stop when childhood is over. If we're wise, we'll continue learning throughout our lives. As I tell my children, they can be told not to do something, but the best lessons they will ever learn are those that come through their own mistakes. My hope and prayer is that they will have a friend who stands close and candidly helps them learn the lessons God is teaching—to both of them!

That's my prayer for all of us. I don't think we ever get to a point in our lives when we don't need friends. I strongly believe God teaches us through other people, and so often those other people are our Heart Sisters. May we be excellent students—and teachers.

Turning to God

Who has been loyal to you throughout your life? Take a moment to thank God for this precious blessing. Who have you been loyal to? Ask God to reveal a friend you can encourage today so that she knows you're there, no matter what. Thank God for the precious gift of friendship.

DAY 5: FINDING AND NURTURING OUR HEART SISTERS

Thirteen years ago, I was very pregnant with my first child and a little bit of a grouch. I was a month away from delivery, and let me tell you, I think I might have hissed at anyone who crossed my path. Hell hath no fury like a pregnant woman in her ninth month.

My sweet husband had been trying to figure out what to do with his dental practice for quite a while. At the time, he was working for a company that placed dentists in the offices they owned, but my husband wanted to have the freedom and control of owning his own business. He knew it would be best if he could find a partner because then it would be possible to take a day off now and then. He had searched for some time, but we knew it was on God's timetable and not our own.

It was a cold January evening as I waited for him at our favorite Chinese restaurant. We were meeting for dinner before our first birthing class at the hospital.

"I think I might have found the practice I want to join," he shared.

I was quite excited because you know what really appeals to pregnant women? Stability. The nesting instinct is no joke.

But then he proceeded to share the details, and suddenly I found myself none too thrilled or excited for us.

The practice he wanted to join was an hour away from our current home. I knew what that meant. We eventually would be moving, and I was having none of it.

I had grown up in the town where we were living. My family was there. My best friends from high school lived in our same neighborhood. I loved our church. Life was going the way I had planned. In fact, things were going so according to my plan that I didn't even consider for one second what God's plan was for us. I told God my plan, invited Him to join me, and then expected Him to approve.

When God didn't approve my plan, I was mad. It was no different than a two-year-old throwing a temper tantrum when she's told she can't have any candy from the grocery store checkout aisle.

"That's fine if that's the practice you want to join, honey, but I'm not moving there," I told him ever-so-lovingly.

My husband is a very wise and smart man, so he knew to pause that discussion until I wasn't so fat and sassy. However, it became obvious we needed to make some changes when our daughter was eighteen months old and our second child was on the way. By that point, I had resigned from my teaching position. There was no longer any reason for us to continue living an hour away from my husband's workplace.

Eventually, I agreed to move fifteen minutes north of our hometown, which would just be a forty-five-minute commute for him. How unselfish of me. Later I agreed to move thirty minutes north of our hometown. Are you so overwhelmed by my generosity right now?

Then one day I looked my tired husband in the eyes and saw how much he was juggling. I was disgusted by my inability to see how working so hard combined with a long commute and little time with his daughter was wearing on him. I agreed to move to the community where he was practicing dentistry. It only took two years for me to arrive at that conclusion. Have I told you I'm a slow learner?

By the time we sold our home and purchased a new one, I was due any day with our second child. Remember how I get in my ninth month of pregnancy? This one was no different from my first one. Ten days after the moving vans pulled out of our driveway, our little Samuel entered the world three weeks early. Not to mention, Jason was new to his dental practice and had to work very hard to make ends meet. His hours were long.

There I was in a new community with a two-year-old and a newborn. I knew no one. The days were very long and very exhausting. I was lonely. I longed for my friends who lived in our former community. I was grieving. I wanted to be near my family again.

And I was frustrated with God—why couldn't He have led Jason to a practice in our former town so we didn't have to uproot everything? Why couldn't He just go along with my plan?

For years I had prayed for God to bring women who believed in Him into my life. I had no idea He would need to uproot me and disrupt our lives to do just what I had been asking Him to do.

When we're in the midst of a plan that doesn't go our way, it's natural to be disappointed. It's also natural to be frustrated with God and confused by the challenges we're facing.

Recently I had to tell my daughter, Sarah, that she can take only two dance classes instead of three. She's about to start middle school and is involved in our local theater. She's a performer. She wasn't too happy with me because the girl loves to dance. However, I knew three dance classes in addition to play rehearsals and the start of middle school were going to be

> **God sees the big picture. The disappointments we experience now are usually for our benefit later.**

too much. She would be tired, stressed out, and living a life of no margin—at the age of twelve.

I know a thing or two about this. Remember Super Natalie? It must be genetic.

I can see the big picture. Saying yes to too much now, even though we might *want* to say yes to it all, isn't what's best in the long run. In this case, Sarah getting what she wanted would lead to three months of exhaustion—for us all.

God sees the big picture. The disappointments we experience now are usually for our benefit later.

Such was the case when we moved to a new community. Once I emerged from the cloud of late-night feedings and diaper changes, I began to accept the fact that we were going to be a part of this community for at least the next thirty-five years—unless God called us elsewhere, of course. I could either plug in or pull away—and pulling away from friendships didn't sound like much fun to me.

Since I had small children and I needed to get out, a friend told me about a ministry called Mothers of Preschoolers (MOPS). Friend, these were my people. The ladies often showed up at the last minute with spit-up stains on their shoulders, bags under their eyes, and disheveled hair. They went straight to the coffee when they entered the room and then fell into their chairs. Yes, my people indeed.

We met every other week, and after a while, we started to get together for playdates. Our children became friends, and let me tell you, nothing forces you past the pretty front porch of relationships quicker than a toddler! Having toddlers around guarantees you'll be escorting many people into your messy living room! These women became my Heart Sisters. They are exactly the women I had prayed for years before.

If you want to find Heart Sisters, assess your season of life. Do you have young children? Seek out a group like MOPS or ask another woman with young children to get together for a playdate. Do you work full-time? Explore the option of evening Bible studies or opportunities to volunteer with an organization that ignites your passion. Are you retired and living in a new city? Find ways to plug in at a new church or assess how you can best volunteer in the community.

Finding Heart Sisters takes courage, friend. Our lonely hearts long to connect with other women, but sometimes the lies begin to shout in the backs of our minds. *What if she doesn't like me? What if she's just too busy? What if she would rather spend time with other friends?*

Those insecurities are not truths from God. What if she *does* like you? What if she isn't too busy but, like you, is lonely and longing for authentic friendship? What if she would love to get to know you as well?

It takes courage to change our situations. Sometimes it feels safer and just plain easier to remain where it's comfortable; but in the long run, it's worth the risk.

Read 1 Samuel 25:1-13. Who is involved in these passages?

What do we know about Nabal?

What do we know about Abigail?

What did Abigail's husband refuse to do for David and his men?

How did David plan to retaliate?

Now read verses 14-35. What did Abigail have the courage to do, and what was the result?

Finally, read verses 36-44. How did the story end?

I'm awestruck by Abigail's courage. It was uncommon for a woman to go against the wishes of her husband and defy his headship; however, in this case, had she not intervened, innocent people from the home of Nabal would have been struck down by David and his men. Nabal's decision to treat an anointed servant of God with such disdain and evil would have had dire consequences. Abigail knew this and, for the greater good of them all, took action.

We will need to have Abigail's courage if we want to have Heart Sisters. We'll have to take matters into our own hands. We'll have to put ourselves "out there" with a willingness to be vulnerable. And we'll have to choose to be a little uncomfortable now and then for the greater good of the end goal: close, authentic friends.

It also will take courage and resolve to maintain those relationships despite busy schedules, the demands of life, and even conflict. If we don't tend to our Heart Sister friendships, they'll wither and die. Of course, some seasons will be busier than others; however, if we constantly put our Heart Sisters on the back burner, they'll eventually burn out. Handwritten notes, encouraging texts, and lunch/dinner/coffee dates are all great ways to tend to our friendships.

> **If we constantly put our Heart Sisters on the back burner, they'll eventually burn out.**

But what if you've done all of these things and you still find yourself longing for Heart Sisters? I completely understand, friend. I've been there. Remember how many years I prayed for faithful, God-loving Heart Sisters?

Waiting for God's timing can be exasperating and frustrating, but God expects us to grow while we wait. When I look back to the years I prayed for godly Heart Sisters, I can see that my relationship with God needed tending before I could tend to my earthly relationships. If we cultivate our relationship with God, our relationships with other people will become healthier and more authentic.

Waiting for God's timing reminds me so much of Jesus' mother, Mary. She knew she was carrying the Messiah, yet for nine months she waited and trusted—not really understanding the full magnitude of God's plan or what would eventually become of her child.

Though waiting can be lonely, if we desire something that God deems as good *according to His plan for us* and we remain faithful to Him, we can be confident that we will be granted those desires.

Reread our memory verse for the week, Psalm 37:4, and write or summarize it below:

Scripture Challenge

Waiting on God's timing isn't easy, but it's worth it! Check out these biblical benefits for waiting on the Lord: Psalms 25:5; 33:20; 123:2; 145:15-16; Isaiah 30:18; Lamentations 3:24-26; 1 Corinthians 4:5; James 5:7-8.

Of course, this does not mean God will give us a fancy car or a big house if we just desire those things in our hearts. However, if we desire things that God would see as fruitful according to His plan for our lives, such as Heart Sister relationships, then they will be ours if we remain faithful to Him. But they will happen on His timetable, not our own.

Sweet sister, I have loved walking this journey with you. I pray it has been a time of growth, encouragement, and support for your heart. I know it has been for mine.

My desire for you and all of God's daughters is to be connected to one another. If we can foster a culture of love, support, and kindness among women, then eventually it will become our default mode. Competition, unkindness, and comparison would become things of the past. Doesn't that sound wonderful? Let's make it happen one Heart Sister at a time, my friend. This revolution will benefit not only us but also generations of women to come. Titus 2:3 tells the older women to teach the younger women "what is good." When we model love and support in our relationships with other women, younger generations will see it—resulting in positive, lasting Kingdom impact. Now that's the work of God!

Turning to God

Take a moment to reflect on today's lesson. What has spoken to you and why? What can you do today to either put yourself out there and meet some Heart Sisters or foster one of your existing friendships? How can you have courage like Abigail this week? Ask God for the necessary strength to have the courage you need. Then sit back and watch His beautiful plan unfold! I would love to close us in prayer:

Dear Lord, thank You for my sister, your daughter, who has completed this study. She is a woman after Your own heart. She understands the importance of living in community with other women, and she desires to do it well. She longs for authentic relationships—relationships

You intend us to have. And she wants to honor You in how she loves, encourages, and supports others. I pray for peace in her heart, for the courage she'll need to reach out to other women, and for relationships that will encourage her to grow closer to You. Lord, we love You so much, and are so thankful for the abundant blessings You've poured over us. Amen.

HEART SISTERS DO'S AND DON'TS

The best way to _____ a good Heart Sister is to _____ a good Heart Sister.

When we mess up, it's what we do _____ that is most important.

A Heart Sister does not _____.

Your honor comes from _____. What other people say or think about you is

_____ as long as you know you are pleasing Him.

My salvation and my honor depend on God;
*   he is my mighty rock, my refuge.*
Trust in him at all times, you people;
*   pour out your hearts to him,*
*   for God is our refuge.*

(Psalm 62:7-8 NIV)

If someone is talking about you, that's really between _____ and the

_____—not the talker and you.

Judging Others

For in the same way you judge others, you will be judged, and with the measure you use, it will be measured to you.

(Matthew 7:2 NIV)

A Heart Sister is a loyal _____ ___ _____.

Rizpah's Loyalty and Prayers

Rizpah daughter of Aiah took sackcloth and spread it out for herself on a rock. From the beginning of the harvest till the rain poured down from the heavens on the bodies, she did not let the birds touch them by day or the wild animals by night.

(2 Samuel 21:10 NIV)

Notes

Week 1

1. Gale Berkowitz, "UCLA Study of Friendship Among Women," *Scribd.*, www.scribd.com/doc/16043143/Ucla-Study-on-Friendship-Among-Women, accessed June 29, 2016.
2. John Mariani, "Shaking Up the Salt Myth," *New York Daily News*, November 24, 2011, www.nydailynews.com/opinion/shaking-salt-myth-thanksgiving-pour -sodium-chloride-article-1.982027, accessed June 29, 2016.
3. *SaltWorks*, "Salt Uses and Tips," www.saltworks.us/salt_info/salt-uses-and -tips.asp.
4. J. D. Barry, D. Mangum, D. R. Brown, M. S. Heiser, M. Custis, E. Ritzema, D. Bomar, *Faithlife Study Bible* (Mt 17:2) (Bellingham, Wash.: Lexham Press, 2012, 2016).
5. John MacArthur, "John: The Apostle of Love," *Grace to You*, April 14, 2002, https://www.gty.org/resources/sermons/62-1/john-the-apostle-of-love, accessed June 29, 2016.
6. Kim Culbertson, *The Liberation of Max McTrue* (Amazon Digital: BookBaby, 2012).
7. C. S. Lewis, *Selected Literary Essays*, ed. Walter Hooper (Cambridge: Cambridge University Press, 1969), 99.

Week 2

1. Spotify Playlist: https://open.spotify.com/user/1255829460/playlist /2zwP8FlcIUrOGYiH0llPoD.

2. *Qin'ah*, Old Testament Hebrew Lexicon, http://www.biblestudytools.com/lexicons/hebrew/nas/qinah.html.

3. *Merriam-Webster Online Dictionary*, s.v., "Masterpiece," http://www.merriam-webster.com/dictionary/masterpiece, accessed July 6, 2016.

4. Carolyn Roth, *Rooted in God: Interpreting Plans in Bible Lore* (Mustang, Okla.: Tate, 2014), 37.

5. *hamartano´*, Strong's G264, https://www.blueletterbible.org/lang/lexicon/lexicon.cfm?t=kjv&strongs=g264.

6. *Lectio Divina*: Divine Reading, Andy Rau, September 6, 2012, https://www.biblegateway.com/blog/2012/09/lectio-divina-divine-reading/.

7. http://biblehub.com/hebrew/5818.htm, s.v., "Uzziah," accessed July 7, 2016.

8. Anxiety and Depression Association of America, "Facts and Statistics of Anxiety and Depression," www.adaa.org/about-adaa/press-room/facts-statistics.

Week 3

1. Ken Sande, *The Peacemaker*: A *Biblical Guide to Resolving Personal Conflict* (Dartmouth, Mass.: Baker, 2004), 11.

2. Andrew Murray, *With Christ in the School of Prayer: Thoughts on Our Training for the Ministry of Intercession* (New York: Fleming H. Revell, 1885), 170.

3. *aiteo´*, Strong's Concordance 154, http://biblehub.com/greek/154.htm.

4. *Krino/krinete*, Strong's 2919, definition 5b, "to judge," http://biblehub.com/greek/2919.htm, accessed July 13, 2016.

5. C. S. Lewis, "Hamlet: The Prince or the Poem?" in *Selected Literary Essays*, 99.

Week 4

1. Daniel Burke, "From Grief to Grace: Wife of Amish Schoolhouse Shooter Breaks Her Silence," September 29, 2013, http://religion.blogs.cnn.com/2013/09/29/from-grief-to-grace-widow-of-amish-schoolhouse-shooter-breaks-her-silence/.

2. Anne Lamott, *Traveling Mercies: Some Thoughts on Faith* (New York: Knopf Doubleday Publishing Group, 2000), 213.

3. *Merriam-Webster Online Dictionary*, s.v. "Resentment," http://www.merriam-webster.com/dictionary/resentment.

4. Rebecca Nicohols Alonzo and Bob Demoss, *The Devil in Pew Number Seven*: A *True Story* (Carol Stream, IL: Tyndale House, 2010), 248.

Week 5

1.   Madeleine L'Engle, *Walking on Water: Reflections on Faith and Art* (Colorado Springs: WaterBrook, 1980), 140–41.
2.   Graham Cooke, *Approaching the Heart of Prophecy* (Vancouver, Wash.: Brilliant Book House, 2010), 28.

Week 6

1.   A. A. Milne, *The House at Pooh Corner* (London: Puffin Books; reissue edition, 1992), 120.
2.   *Merriam-Webster Online Dictionary*, s.v., "Authentic," www.merriam-webster.com /dictionary/authentic.

More Abingdon Women Bible Studies

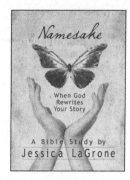

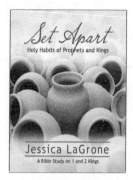

Namesake
978-1-4267-7804-9

Broken and Blessed
978-1-4267-7841-4

Set Apart
978-1-4267-7846-9

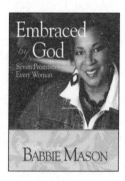

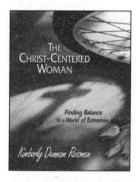

Embraced by God
978-1-4267-7794-3

This I Know For Sure
978-1-4267-7569-7

The Christ-Centered Woman
978-1-4267-7568-0

Each Leader Kit includes one of the following:
participant workbook, leader guide, DVD.
Each component can also be purchased individually.

Learn more at AbingdonWomen.com.

More Abingdon Women Bible Studies

Jeremiah
978-1-4267-8897-0

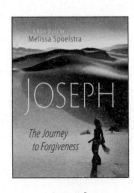

Joseph
978-1-4267-8914-4

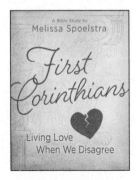

First Corinthians
978-1-5018-0173-0

Beautiful Already
978-1-5018-1359-7

Anonymous
978-1-4267-9218-2

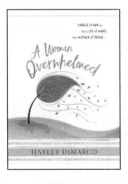

**A Woman
Overwhelmed**
Coming May 2017
978-1-5018-3997-9

Each Leader Kit includes one of the following:
participant workbook, leader guide, DVD.
Each component can also be purchased individually.

Learn more at AbingdonWomen.com.